D0246702
"Yeah, no sweat, this lifejacket definitely looks cooool"

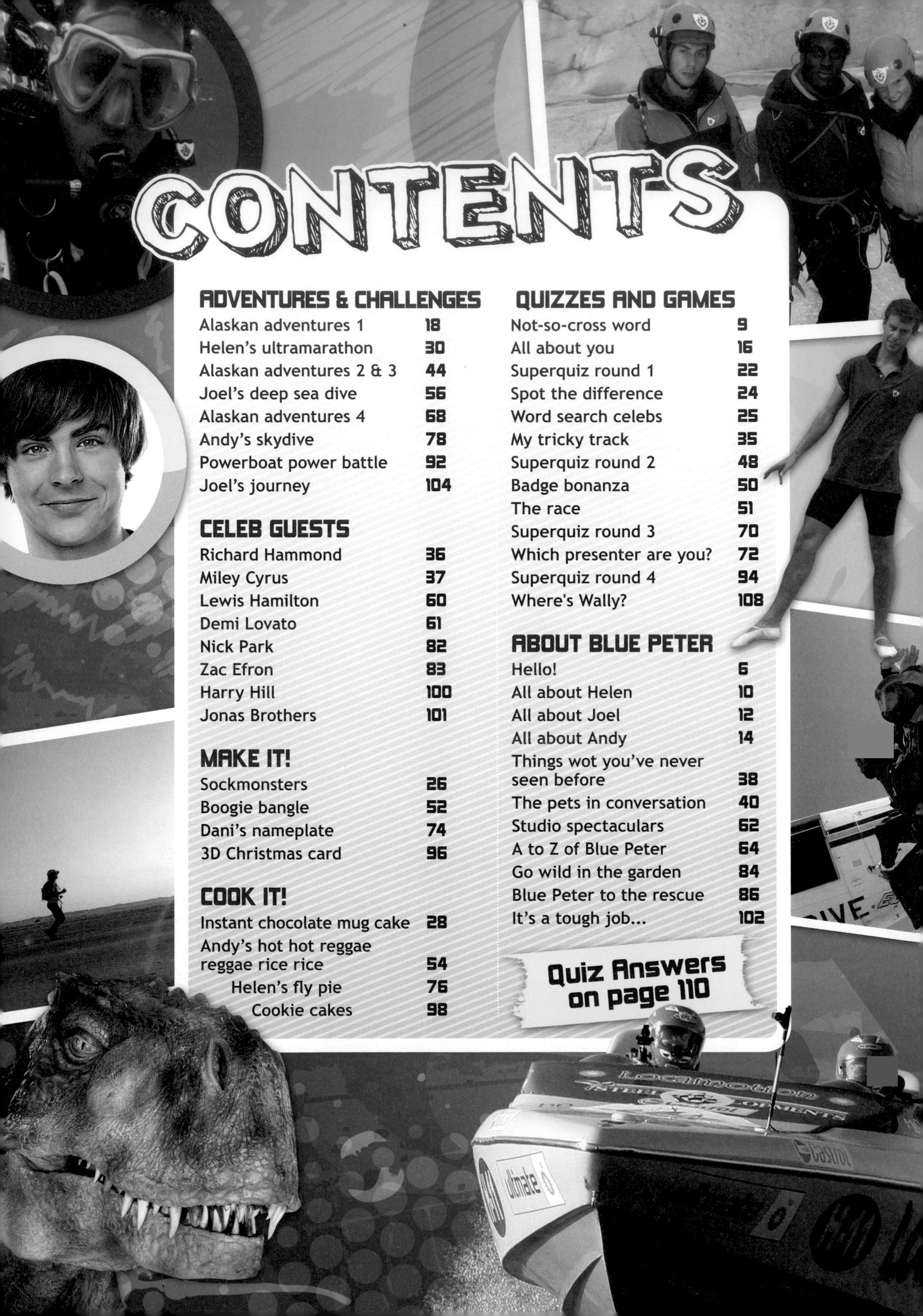

CONTENTS

Quiz Answers on page 110

Published 2009 by Pedigree Books Limited, Beech Hill House, Walnut Gardens, Exeter, Devon, EX4 4DH.
www.pedigreebooks.com • Email: books@pedigreegroup.co.uk By arrangement with the BBC.

Hello...

...AND WELCOME TO OUR BLUE PETER ANNUAL FOR 2010! INTO THESE 112 PAGES OF GOODNESS, WE'VE SQUEEZED AS MANY QUIZZES, GAMES, MAKES, BAKES, ADVENTURES, CELEBS AND STORIES AS WE POSSIBLY COULD.

It's been a packed year for the three of us, and choosing the best bits to include has been a pretty hard job. After all, a book listing all the challenges which Joel and Andy managed to win would run to, oooh, at least a page.

But we've made our final selection, and we really hope you enjoy the highlights. You've got powerboats, moose poo and the world's fastest chocolate cake all to come.

Helen xx

Don't forget

We're on BBC One on Tuesdays and Wednesdays, with more games, things to do and updates 24/7 on the website. Enjoy!

BEIJING COMPETITION

Tayyiba won our Olympic competition, and a superstar role at the Beijing Olympics in front of a TV audience of 3.5 billion people! She represented the UK's children as China handed over the games to London for the 2012 Olympics. And Gareth repeated the trick at the Paralympics. What amazing winners!

With David Beckham and Leona Lewis!

MISSION NUTRITION

Tens of thousands of you got involved in our massive appeal, Mission Nutrition. We asked you to hold bring-and-buy sales to raise money to help children across the world eat and grow better food. And you absolutely didn't let us down. Thanks to you, we're providing over half a million meals for children worldwide! We worked with the charities Save the Children, ContinYou, and the Federation of City Farms and Community Gardens to provide meals, breakfast clubs and gardens in the UK and abroad.

OUR 50TH BIRTHDAY

So it was only, like, the Queen who helped us celebrate our 50th birthday! We're now officially the world's longest-running children's magazine programme, and to mark the occasion she invited us to a special Blue Peter party at Buckingham Palace, together with four amazing viewers to whom she gave Gold Blue Peter Badges.

"Nice place you've got here!"*

The Queen's bakers made a cake featuring some legendary Blue Peter moments...

...including when an elephant pooed in the studio.

And, live on BBC One, we had a party at Television Centre, our home almost ever since day one! Joel drummed with McFly and we let off loads of fireworks. What better way to celebrate?!

*Yes, that is really what Joel said. Maybe he needs lessons in etiquette...

NOT-SO-CROSS WORD

NOW IT'S YOUR TURN! CELEBRATE SOME OF THE BEST MOMENTS OF THE PAST YEAR ON BLUE PETER BY FILLING IN THIS PUZZLE THAT'S (AHEM) RATHER SHIP-SHAPE. RATHER HELPFULLY, WE'VE GIVEN YOU ALL THE ANSWERS ALREADY. YOU HAVE TO FIND THE RIGHT BOX FOR EACH SEPARATE WORD BELOW. EASY? PERHAPS NOT...

(PS: Get started by putting the name of the celeb in the middle in the boxes outlined in red.)

ANSWERS:

FACTBYTE FACTORY
ECO CAR RACE
BOOK AWARDS
TOTEM POLE
SWEET ART
CAMP ROCK
BEE CAFE
T-REX
TAP
WEB

Hugs
Helen
xx

ALL ABOUT HELEN

ME IN FIVE WORDS

Honest, loyal, bubbly, determined, friendly

FUNNIEST TRAIT

I'm not funny. That I'm Northern? Joel finds that funny!

20,000 bees on me!

SECRET OF MY SUCCESS

I wait till the others give up

FAVOURITE PERSON I MET

A Welsh boy who raised money for the Welsh air ambulance

I'D MOST LIKE TO MEET

David Beckham

Most irritating habit: I don't know when to shut up

SCARIEST CHALLENGE IMAGINABLE

To be buried alive with rats

DREAM ADVENTURE

To climb Everest, glide off the top and then husky-sled back to base

FACTBYTES

I SUPPORT: Kilmarnock and Carlisle
I LOVE: Smiley people
I WATCH: Come Dine With Me
I LISTEN TO: Anything
I PLAY: Championship Manager

Hello.

All About Joel

ME IN FIVE WORDS

Ridiculous, embarrassing, hyperactive, impatient, irritating

FUNNIEST TRAIT

Never saying what you expect me to say

SECRET OF MY SUCCESS

Not knowing I have any talent

FAVOURITE PERSON I MET

The Queen

I'D MOST LIKE TO MEET

Arnold Schwarzenegger

Making moose poo earrings in Alaska!

Most irritating habit: I don't think before speaking

In Uganda for Comic Relief

FACTBYTES

I SUPPORT: Fulham
I LOVE: Waking up late
I WATCH: Home and Away
I LISTEN TO: St Vincent
I PLAY: Pro-Evolution Soccer

SCARIEST CHALLENGE IMAGINABLE

Running 78 miles against Helen

DREAM ADVENTURE

To go to space - wearing only a swimming costume

Stay Cool

ALL ABOUT ANDY

Doing a loop the loop!

ME IN FIVE WORDS

Chilled, smiley, sleepy, chatty, fearless

FUNNIEST TRAIT

My laugh - it's a real cackle

SECRET OF MY SUCCESS

My friendliness

FAVOURITE PERSON I MET

Lewis Hamilton

I'D MOST LIKE TO MEET

Nelson Mandela

SCARIEST CHALLENGE IMAGINABLE

To deep sea dive in a cave surrounded by snakes

DREAM ADVENTURE

To trek from the north to the south of Africa

Most irritating habit:
I bite my nails

FACTBYTES

I SUPPORT: Arsenal

I LOVE: Trying out new food

I WATCH: Wolverine & The X-Men

I LISTEN TO: Hip hop jazz

I PLAY: Pro-Evolution Soccer

Turn yourself into the newest Blue Peter presenter! Print out a photo of yourself and stick it on this page. Give yourself a Blue Peter badge too by cutting out the one below. And don't forget to sign your autograph. You rock!

ALL ABOUT

ME IN FIVE WORDS

FUNNIEST TRAIT

SECRET OF MY SUCCESS

Most irritating habit:

FAVOURITE PERSON I MET

I'D MOST LIKE TO MEET

SCARIEST CHALLENGE IMAGINABLE

DREAM ADVENTURE

FACTBYTES

I SUPPORT:

I LOVE:

I WATCH:

I LISTEN TO:

I PLAY:

ADVENTURE 1: GLACIER

THE AMERICAN STATE OF ALASKA IS FAMOUS FOR ITS HUGE LANDSCAPES AND SUPER-SIZED, WELL, EVERYTHING. FOR OUR SUMMER EXPEDITION, WE SET OFF TO DISCOVER EXACTLY WHAT THIS AWESOME PLACE HAD TO OFFER.

"Yeay!"

"We're on a mission to conquer Alaska!"

The Dawes Glacier: an eerie, beautiful place on the southwest coast of Alaska. A massive river of ice that runs thirty miles from the mountains into the sea. As it reaches the water, it is as high as a 33-storey building.

Our challenge: to get as close to it as possible - using two different methods of transport, Helen and Joel in a boat, and Andy in a helicopter.

From the air, Andy was able to see the glacier in all its glory - particularly its striking blue colour. This is a weird but completely natural effect. Light is made up of all the colours of the rainbow, but the reds and yellows have very little energy and are soaked up by ice, especially the thick, pure ice of a glacier. Blue light has more energy and escapes, and so that's the colour you see.

"Yee-ha! This is the way to see the world!"

"Typical! Andy gets the chopper, and us - the slow boat..."

ALASKA
USA
But even from the boat...
"I'm ready for anything"
"Wow!"
First mission accomplished - but our next task was actually to camp on a glacier. Um, easier said than done....
FACTBYTES
• Alaska is six times bigger than the UK
• But its total population is smaller than Leeds

Putting up the tent took us about five times longer than it should have done. But at last it went up. That night, we slept like logs.

After a day's climbing training, our final glacier challenge would be one of the most terrifying things any of us had ever tried.

Moulins are amongst the most dangerous places on earth. They're like huge plugholes in the glacier, allowing melted water from the surface to gush at terrifying speed to the bottom - sometimes 100 metres down.

If you fall inside a moulin without a safety line, it is almost certain death. And one of us was going to climb down one! (Why? Just because you can.)

OUR ALASKAN ADVENTURES CONTINUE ON PAGE 44

Blue Peter Superquiz Round 1

WITH YOUR HOST HELEN SKELTON

How well do you think you know the world's most famous TV show for kids? We've got a whole stack of questions to test you out, so get your brains in gear and get going!

1

I ran 78 miles non-stop through the Namibian desert to complete my ultramarathon in April, but how long did I have to do it?

A. One day
B. Two days
C. One week

2

Where did we go for our summer expedition in 2008?

A. Alaska
B. Australia
C. Austria

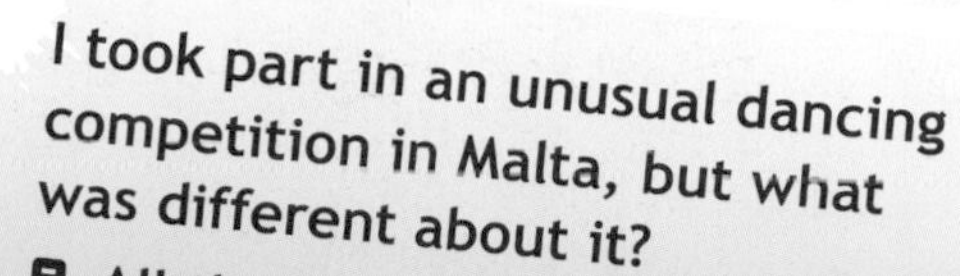

3 I was lucky enough to change the time on one of Britain's most famous clocks, Big Ben, but what exactly is Big Ben the name of?

A. The man who looks after it
B. The massive bell inside
C. The railway station nearby

4 Which English county was I born in?

____

5 How many times a week is Blue Peter on BBC One?

A. Once
B. Twice
C. Three times

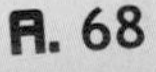

6 When we set a new pancake-tossing world record in the studio, how many flips did chef Aldo Zilli manage in a minute?

A. 68
B. 117
C. 267

Record!

7 I took part in an unusual dancing competition in Malta, but what was different about it?

A. All the dresses were made of metal
B. We danced underwater
C. My partner was in a wheelchair

8 We met the rare breed of dog which US President Barack Obama bought for his children, but what is its name?

A. British bulldog
B. Portuguese water dog
C. German shepherd dog

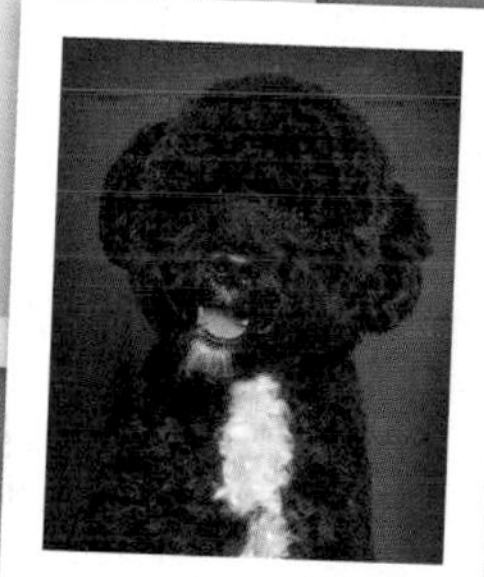

9 Andy and I discovered Britain's oldest children's film, "The Match Seller", but in what year was it made?

A. 1902
B. 1935
C. 1957

10 I spent a day working as an air stewardess at the UK's newest airport terminal, Terminal Five, but at which UK airport is it based?

A. London Heathrow
B. Glasgow
C. Manchester

My score out of 10:

Turn to page 110 for the answers

SPOT THE DIFFERENCE

YOU KNOW THE SCORE. TWO PHOTOS, APPARENTLY IDENTICAL - BUT LOOK MORE CLOSELY, AND YOU'LL SEE WE'VE HIDDEN A WHOLE SERIES OF CUNNING CHANGES. IN TOTAL, THERE ARE TEN CHANGES BETWEEN THE TOP AND BOTTOM IMAGES. SEE IF YOU CAN GET THEM ALL.

The answers, should you need them, are on page 110.

WORD SEARCH CELEBS

IT'S BEEN AN INCREDIBLE YEAR ON BLUE PETER. IT SEEMS LIKE EVERYONE WHO'S ANYONE HAS BEEN ON THE SHOW. AND IT'S NOT JUST US SAYING IT. SEE FOR YOURSELF BY COMPLETING OUR FIENDISH WORDSEARCH WITH A TWIST.

The first name runs in a straight line, but the surname goes off at an angle. We've done Megan Fox already,to give you the idea. See if you can get the remaining 14.

- DAVID BECKHAM
- MILEY CYRUS
- SCOOBY DOO
- ZAC EFRON
- RICHARD HAMMOND
- HARRY HILL
- CHRIS HOY
- SHIA LABEOUF
- LEONA LEWIS
- DEMI LOVATO
- THE QUEEN
- GEORGE SAMPSON
- EMMA WATSON
- JACQUELINE WILSON

J	F	A	E	M	Z	H	H	C	L	A	U	R	L
A	U	T	S	B	A	A	H	Y	L	M	E	H	E
C	O	P	O	M	R	R	C	E	F	R	O	N	O
Q	E	L	M	R	I	N	B	I	Y	T	R	E	N
U	B	E	Y	S	T	L	S	S	I	W	E	L	A
E	A	H	H	C	N	H	E	G	E	O	R	G	E
L	L	I	E	O	A	S	E	Y	C	Y	R	U	S
I	A	L	S	O	Y	Q	D	Q	U	E	E	N	A
N	S	L	M	B	T	W	E	A	R	T	T	K	M
E	I	D	F	Y	D	O	O	G	V	H	R	J	P
W	L	I	M	E	D	A	S	D	F	I	G	M	S
P	O	P	E	G	M	E	W	F	C	G	D	B	O
C	V	A	G	T	I	M	A	H	K	C	E	B	N
N	A	E	A	I	X	T	A	W	A	T	S	O	N
M	T	E	N	O	D	R	Y	S	W	L	H	E	M
B	O	V	F	C	D	H	A	M	M	O	N	D	P

You will need:

- An old sock
- Cotton wool or soft toy stuffing
- Buttons
- Needle & thread
- Scissors

SOCKMONSTERS

Making sockmonsters with Corrie's Sophie and Chesney on the set of the legendary soap.

STAGE 1

Lay the sock on the table and shape the heel into lips. Sew in a border to make the lips stick out. (You might want to get an adult to help out - particularly if you want to offload the needlework on someone else!)

Create the eyes by sewing buttons above the lips. The more eyes, the weirder it will look.

STAGE 2

MAKE IT

WE TOTALLY LOVE THESE GUYS! WEIRD-LOOKING SOFT TOYS ARE A TOP TRENDY BUY IN THE SHOPS - BUT THEY NORMALLY COST £20 OR MORE. YOU CAN MAKE THEM FOR FREE, AND THEY MAKE MEMORABLE PRESENTS TOO!

STAGE 3

Start making the alien antennae by cutting from the top of the sock to about halfway down. Then cut off a snippet about 4cm from the bottom of the sock.

STAGE 4

Take that snippet and cut it in half downwards - these will be the arms. Now cut upwards from the bottom of the sock to about 2 cms under the lips - these will be the legs.

STAGE 5

Take each arm, turn it inside out and sew along the long edge only. Then turn the whole sock inside out and sew up all the edges, leaving a 2cm gap on either side so you can put the stuffing in.

STAGE 6

Turn the monster back the right way round and stuff the monster with cotton wool or soft toy stuffing through the small hole you left. When you've finished, sew up the gap, sew on the arms - and, hey presto, your sock monster is complete!

TOP TIPS:

- We loved making soccer sockmonsters (geddit?!) by using some of our old footie socks.
- Give your monster even more of a face with white felt for teeth and red felt for a tongue.

INSTANT CHOCOLATE MUG CAKE

You will need:

- 2 tbsp self-raising flour
- 2 tbsp cocoa
- 1 egg white
- 2 tbsp milk
- 1 large mug
- 2 tbsp caster sugar
- 2 tbsp vegetable oil

IF YOU'RE ANYTHING LIKE US, YOU'LL LOVE CHOCOLATE. AND, MAYBE LIKE US TOO, YOU SOMETIMES CAN'T BE BOTHERED TO SPEND TOO LONG COOKING EITHER. SO THIS HAS GOT TO BE THE MOST PERFECT RECIPE EVER! THREE MINUTES AND IT'S DONE. IN FACT, IT'S SO EASY WE THOUGHT WE'D ALL HAVE A GO AND SEE WHOSE CAKE CAME OUT BEST. GUESS WHO WON...

BAKE IT

STEP 1

Measure out all your ingredients. Smile!

STEP 2

Mix the flour, sugar and cocoa together in the mug.

STEP 3

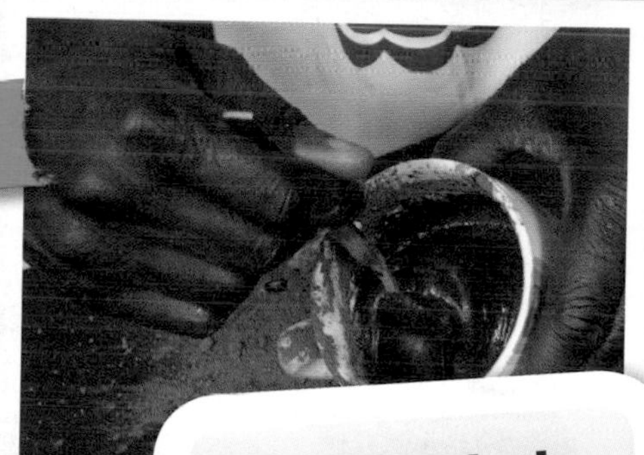

Mix in the egg, milk and oil. (See, it's really not hard...)

Andy - what a mess!

STEP 4

Put your mug in the microwave and cook on full power for three minutes.

STEP 5

The mug will be hot, so wear oven gloves to get it out of the microwave. (We're struggling to make it any more complicated than this!)

STEP 6

Turn the mug upside down and tip the cake out. Turn it back the right way up again. Compare how you've done with your friend. Eat!

You could decorate or ice it - like when we made it at Easter with Dr Who assistant Michelle Ryan.

HELEN'S ULTRAMARATHON

IT'S HARD TO SAY EXACTLY HOW I FELT WHEN I FIRST DECIDED TO TAKE ON MY ULTIMATE CHALLENGE: THE NAMIBIA ULTRAMARATHON. TRYING TO RUN 78 MILES IN 24 HOURS THROUGH THE HEAT OF THE AFRICAN DESERT WOULD BE THE TOUGHEST THING I'D EVER DONE IN MY LIFE. BUT I'M NOT A NATURAL RUNNER, AND HADN'T QUITE REALISED HOW TOUGH THE FIRST FOUR MONTHS OF TRAINING WOULD BE....

I'm just a glutton for punishment!

It all began early in January with my very first race: the 10-mile "Rough 'n' Tumble" through the steep, muddy hills of Wiltshire. At the time, I thought it was hard going. Now, it seems like a walk in the park.

As I collapsed over the finish line, there was a huge surprise waiting for me. Rory, my trainer, came up and told me I had to run the whole thing again. The whole thing again! I didn't think it was possible. But he told me that, if I was really to complete my 78 mile ultimate challenge, I needed to be able to slog on. So I started off again, slowly, one foot in front of the other. And, painful though it was, I made it.

For the next four months, I trained for several hours almost every day. And took on a series of preparation challenges that just seemed to get bigger and bigger.

The unglamorous side of running: endless hours in the gym

"MY" LONDON MARATHON

I did my first full marathon, all 26.2 miles of it, through the streets of London. That's over 42km! It took me a while, mind - over five hours. But Rory says that, if I'm to do my 78 miles, it's not about how fast I go, but whether I get there in the end.

"Aww, do I have to?"

DARING DOUBLE

One of my hardest moments: two marathons in two days through the biting snow. It wasn't easy, but I did it. Don't think this is mad, but, despite the pain, I was actually really enjoying this.

Namibia, ready or not, here I come...

HOMETOWN 50-MILER

I loved this one! I've always supported Carlisle United, so I ran 30 miles to their ground, Brunton Park, and then 20 miles round and round the track. That's 50 miles in one day! Even Andy and Joel came to run a lap with me - thanks guys.

THE NAMIBIA ULTRAMARATHON

06:05 19°C: Finally, the big day dawns. All that preparation, all that training. Will it be enough?

07:10 22°C: I eat breakfast, get my kit together and do a few vital health checks. And then...

09:00 25°C 0 miles: We're off! 23 runners. I'm actually feeling quite nervous, but relieved to be on the way.

10:25 29°C 6 miles: This is going well, and I'm actually enjoying it. But the rocky ground is worrying me - it's harder to run on than I imagined. And the heat is rising.

12:42 35°C 13 miles CHECKPOINT 1: The first shock. The heat is hitting people harder than anyone expected. Three runners drop out, including the guy who finished second last year.

15:05 43°C 19 miles: The afternoon heat is unbelievable. I'm feeling totally whacked by it. I can't do much more than walk. I feel like I'm drinking and eating all the right things, but none of it seems to be making a difference. Other people are dropping out and I'm worried I might be next.

16:10 42°C 21 miles: I collapse on the ground. The support crew try to cool me down, and one massages my legs to stop my muscles seizing up. Eventually I get up and struggle on. But I'm not sure I'm ever going to get to Checkpoint 2.

17:40 31°C 26 miles CHECKPOINT2: Getting here is a massive relief. I recover here for an hour. And as it gets dark, it starts to cool down, which is helping.

19:37 25°C 31 miles: I'm feeling a bit better and begin to pick up speed. My feet are beginning to hurt, though.

22:15 21°C 39 miles CHECKPOINT 3: It's like a warzone: there are just 15 runners left. One is on a drip, another is being sick. I take off my trainers and am shocked to see my feet covered in blisters.

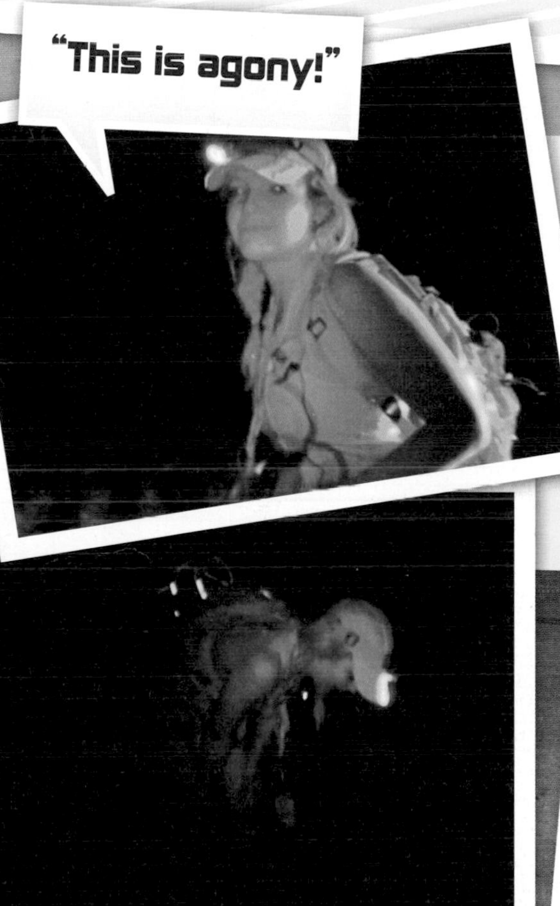

23:45 16°C 43 miles: I'm in total agony. I don't think I can carry on. With every step, it feels like someone is putting razor blades on my feet. The race doctor drives up and gives me emergency treatment. I'm battling with myself. But the idea of quitting is even worse than the pain in my feet. I summon up every last drop of willpower, and stagger on.

03:06 13°C 52 miles CHECKPOINT 4: I've made it to the next checkpoint! But I've lost so much time, I'm warned I might not finish within 24 hours. Unbelievably, I have to pick up the pace.

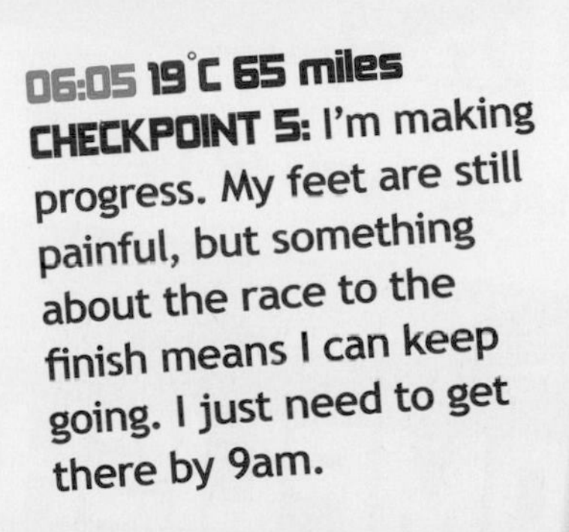

06:05 19°C 65 miles CHECKPOINT 5: I'm making progress. My feet are still painful, but something about the race to the finish means I can keep going. I just need to get there by 9am.

08:50 19°C 78 miles THE FINISH. I've done it - with ten minutes to spare! I'm one of just 12 finishers, and only the second woman ever, to complete this race! I can't believe what the last 24 hours have been like: there were two points when I thought I might have to quit. But for me, failure was not an option.

After I crossed the finish line, there was one more surprise waiting for me...

I'm really proud of what I managed to achieve. I'm also thankful to Blue Peter viewers for all your messages, support and encouragement. I know that it's with your help that I managed to get through this ultimate challenge.

MISSION ACCOMPLISHED!

MY TRICKY TRACK

SO I COMPLETED MY 78 MILES. NOW CAN YOU ANSWER MY CUNNING **RUNNING-RELATED QUESTIONS** TO GET ALL THE WAY ROUND THIS TRACK? THE FIRST AND LAST LETTERS OF EACH WORD ARE THE SAME. AND IF YOU PICK OUT THE HIGHLIGHTED LETTERS IN ORDER, THEY SPELL THE NAME OF THE **ULTIMATE CHALLENGE** I WOULD LOVE TO TAKE ON NEXT.

Put this letter in the first box below

CLUES

1. The African country where I did my run (7 letters)
2. The country which hosted the 2004 Olympic Games (6)
3. The medal you get for coming second (6)
4. A race in which runners pass a baton to each other (5)
5. The colour of t-shirt I wore on the second morning of my run (6)
6. I had to do a lot of this when my feet ached (it's also a slow track event) (7)
7. On your marks, get set... What? (2)
8. The second name of current British female Olympic 400m champion. First name Christina. Tricky, this one. It rhymes with "ohuruogu" (clue: that's a pretty big clue) (8)
9. The type of marathon I did (5)
10. The general name for all kinds of track and field activities (9)
11. What made it get so hot in the Namibian desert (3)

My ideal next ultimate challenge:

THE SOLUTION IS ON PAGE 110.

CELEB GUEST: RICHARD HAMMOND

FACTBYTES:

FULL NAME: Richard Mark Hammond
JOB: TV presenter
DOB: 19 December 1969

ON BLUE PETER:
Richard made explosions using household chemicals

HE TOLD US:
- If I invented a car, it would run on sweets and I'd call it the Velociraptor
- Ham, cheese and pickle is my favourite sandwich!

BET YOU DIDN'T KNOW:
Richard failed his first driving test when he jumped a red light - whoops!

ON HIS JOB:
"Being a TV presenter has its difficult bits, the easy bits, the fun bits and dangerous bits. I'm lucky to do it, I know."

WHEN HE WAS YOUNGER:
"I wanted to be a wildlife presenter. It's still something I'd love to do, but I think I may have left it too late. Mind you, I also wanted to be a spaceman..."

"I've always been interested in why things do what they do around us. Anything from 'Why does my tummy feel funny when I take a hard left in the car?' Whatever the question, science generally has an answer for it."

"Your friends are the people who will always love you and be there for you. Be as close to them as possible: they are like a shield, amour around you, something that can protect you."

CELEB GUEST:

MILEY CYRUS

FACTBYTES:

FULL NAME: Destiny Hope Cyrus
JOB: Actress and singer
DOB: 23 November 1992

ON BLUE PETER:
Miley did a quickfire personality quiz

SHE TOLD US:
- I don't ever brush my hair - my wonderful hair stylist looks after it
- "The Climb" is my favourite song

BET YOU DIDN'T KNOW:
Miley prefers singing to acting, brown to blonde hair and dogs to cats.

ON HER JOB:
"I love working with my dad, coz it's nice to have someone that unconditionally loves me, and he is always there for me and is very supportive."

WHEN SHE WAS YOUNGER:
"I studied mostly by watching other people. Don't replicate people you admire, but find moments that draw them to you, and try to have moments like those yourself."

THINGS WOT YOU'VE NEVER SEEN BEFORE!

A REAL CASTLE OF SAND

When Andy heard about some of the world's biggest sandcastles in Holland, he just had to go and help out.

To make these massive creations, the sculptors don't use sand from the beach. Sea erosion means the miniscule grains are too circular (imagine building with marbles). Instead they bring in sand from a nearby river, as it's more like tiny building blocks.

These sculptures don't use any glue!

JOEL DOING BALLET

No, we never thought we'd see this either. For some reason, Joel got it into his head that he would be good at ballet – and amazingly, he was right. His slender (all right, skinny) body meant he could do the leaps and turns perfectly.

"I'm quite enjoying this really!"

He went on stage to play a part in the English National Ballet's Angelina Ballerina. And did brilliantly.

Joel doin' his thang!

LIGHT PAINTING

This amazing new artistic trend from Germany is based on waving a coloured torch while taking a very long photo, and using the blurry lines to create a picture.

But it's not quick. Making this version of "The Very Hungry Caterpillar" took Andy all night!

The caterpillar starts his attack...

STONE BALANCING

Another eye-defying spectacle! These stones aren't held together with glue; instead they are just balanced on top of each other. By placing them with incredible care, you can find what's called the "centre of gravity": the point at which they no longer topple over.

"How did I do that?!"

Helen tried it out in the Blue Peter garden, and, although she failed with a large-ish stone, incredibly, she managed it with something a bit smaller. That girl is too good to be true!

THE PETS IN CONVERSATION

The Blue Peter pets are stars week-in week-out on Blue Peter. But we don't often get to hear from them in person. So for this year's Annual, they kindly agreed to sit down and have an exclusive chat. Here's what they told us.

MABEL

HELLO - HOW ARE YOU TODAY?
I'm fine thanks! I've been swimming, and I absolutely love to swim. Whenever I get in the water, it always turns into a mini-adventure, so I had lots and lots of fun.

IS SWIMMING YOUR MAIN LOVE?
Actually no. I love balls more than anything else. If ever there's a ball in the studio, I just have to chase it. The presenters sometimes get a bit annoyed if I walk right across their shot.

THAT SOUNDS VERY FUNNY!
Yes, you've reminded me of when rugby star Jonny Wilkinson came on the show. He set up to kick his rugby ball, but I grabbed it before he could stop me and ran off with it. It caused total chaos!

IS THERE ANYTHING YOU DON'T LIKE ABOUT BEING IN THE BLUE PETER STUDIO?
I don't like big bangs. Sometimes, when a presenter has completed a challenge, everyone cheers and that freaks me out. When we had the huge T-Rex in the studio, that scared me a lot - its roaring and movement were totally realistic. There are some dogs I know that wouldn't have coped with it at all. I just hid at the back of the studio until it went away.

"This is me, with my very own sculpture in the Blue Peter garden."

DO YOU GET ON WITH THE PRESENTERS?
Of course! Helen's a real doggy person, so I find it very easy being with her. Joel is surprisingly friendly. He comes up and hugs me - normally when I'm not expecting it. And Andy - who doesn't love Andy? He's so friendly and always makes sure I'm included in any of the games they're playing.

DO YOU MIND THE ATTENTION?
Sometimes I don't like it. It takes me a while to trust people. I'm glad that there isn't a Hello magazine for the doggy world. I'd hate it.

WHAT'S BEEN THE HIGHLIGHT OF YOUR TIME ON BLUE PETER?
Do you know the film director John Lasseter? He's created Toy Story, Cars, Nemo, all of those films. When he did Bolt, he came on the show and drew a cartoon version of me. I've been on the show for 12 years, but that was a very special moment, I don't mind telling you.

LUCY

WHAT'S GOING ON?
Oh, I'm so busy, but I love it! My top priority is making sure I'm on top form for all the Blue Peter shows. But then I also make quite a few public appearances.

SUCH AS?
I opened a church fair recently. That was great. Imagine having your face and name on the posters. There aren't many dogs who can say that. And I love going into schools and meeting children. I never get tired of children stroking me, and sometimes I wag my tail so much I think it's going to drop off!

HOW DO YOU COPE WITH THE ATTENTION?
To be honest, I've had it all my life. I've been on Blue Peter since I was a puppy, and whenever celebrities come onto the show, they always want their photo taken with me. I haven't known anything different. Mabel doesn't like it that much, though, so I have to protect her sometimes.

DO YOU TWO GET ON?
Hugely! We are such great friends. And we love the cats and Shelley too. It's a bit of a cliché, but I suppose we are just one big happy family.

YOU'RE CLEARLY A BIT OF A PRO. HAS ANYTHING EVER FREAKED YOU OUT OR GONE WRONG IN THE BLUE PETER STUDIO?
Once, we had locusts in the studio, and I stuck my head in the tank and got covered in them. I didn't like that. And as for things going wrong - when does that not happen? Did you see the episode when we got washed by Helen and Andy?

YES.
Well that didn't go according to plan, did it? Mabel turned round and had her bottom facing the camera. Not a pretty sight! And I ran off at the first possible opportunity, shaking water everywhere.

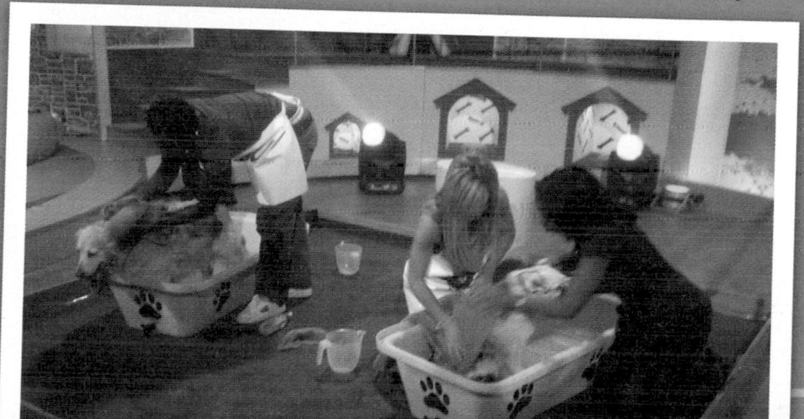

DID THAT GET YOU INTO TROUBLE?
Not really. Helen, Joel and Andy are quite used to me, and they know I'm pretty laidback most of the time. Some dogs bark a lot near other animals, but I just love it when they come into the studio. One time we had a llama in - that was great. Overall, I think I was born to be a Blue Peter dog.

SHELLEY

THIS IS YOUR FIRST-EVER INTERVIEW, ISN'T IT?
Actually, I think it is. I've been on the show for five years, but I don't get as much attention as the other pets.

DO YOU MIND?
Not really. What matters to me is being well looked after and loved, and I certainly get that.

SO DO YOU LIKE BEING ON BLUE PETER?
I love it! Of course, I hibernate for around two months each winter, so I miss quite a few programmes. I've never experienced a Christmas show, for instance. The others tell me about it, and it sounds wonderful.

WHEN YOU'RE NOT HIBERNATING, WHERE DO YOU SLEEP?
Under an old casserole dish in the garden. It makes a lovely cave!

SHELLEY, DON'T TAKE THIS THE WRONG WAY, BUT HOW OLD ARE YOU?
Don't worry - people ask me that all the time. No one knows for sure, but I'm definitely in my twenties. That's still quite young for a tortoise of course.

WERE YOU BORN IN THE UK?
No, Morocco. I'm a Mediterranean Spur Thigh tortoise, otherwise known as a Testudo Gracea. I was brought illegally into Britain, and rescued as an adult.

WOW, THAT SOUNDS LIKE QUITE A STORY!
Yes it is. I might write a book about it one day.

YOU SHOULD. WE'D READ IT.
Thank you. I've only clocked up five years on Blue Peter so far, but I hope to be going for many more to come.

SOCKS

WE WERE TOLD BY LUCY THAT YOU ALL GET ON BRILLIANTLY. IS THAT THE TRUTH?
I adore Lucy. I would like to get a bit closer to Mabel sometimes, but she's not so keen on that. Lucy's right, though. Overall we do get on famously.

TALKING OF FAMOUS, YOU ARE ONE OF BRITAIN'S TOP CELEBRITY CATS. WHAT'S THAT LIKE?
I don't think of it like that. I'm a normal ragdoll cat who lives a mostly normal life and just happens to appear on TV sometimes. I've got other cats as friends at home, and I suppose they keep me grounded.

BUT YOU MUST LIKE THE ATTENTION?
Yes, I suppose I do. I love getting all the cuddles and hugs!

COOKIE

YOU'RE THE NEWEST PET. DO YOU OFTEN FEEL LIKE THE JUNIOR PARTY?
Actually, I think I'm a bit cheekier than Socks. Of the two of us, I'm most likely to go walkabout in the studio. Which drives Helen, Joel and Andy mad, because I keep wandering out of shot.

DO THEY TRY TO STOP YOU?
Well they do, but they've also got to concentrate on what they're saying, so it's quite easy to slip out of their hands.

WHO IS YOUR FAVOURITE PRESENTER?
Joel has tried really hard to get to know me better. I do appreciate that. If you're reading this Joel, keep it up! But he still jumps around too

YOU ALWAYS LOOK SO GOOD. DO YOU HAVE SPECIAL HAIR AND MAKE-UP BEFORE APPEARING ON TV?
I'm groomed every day to keep me healthy and make sure my coat is free of knots and tangles. But that's standard practice for all ragdolls. I've got a thicker coat than Cookie, and it takes much longer to groom me, but I don't do anything extra for TV.

DO YOU EVER GET TIMES WHEN YOU DON'T LIKE BEING ON SET?
Sometimes. I think I'm a bit more shy than Cookie, even though I'm older. And I don't like it when it gets too noisy.

ONE HIGHLIGHT FROM YOUR TIME ON BLUE PETER, PLEASE SOCKS.
When Star Wars actor Ewan McGregor cuddled me. Now that's something to tell my grandchildren!

much, and can be really noisy. I suppose, if you pushed me, I'd say I liked Helen the best.

WHAT'S THE NAUGHTIEST THING YOU'VE DONE ON THE SHOW?
One time there were loads of artificial flowers on the set, and I couldn't stop chewing them! That was quite bad.

OK. QUICKFIRE ROUND. FAVOURITE FOOD?
Fresh raw minced beef.

CAN YOU DO ANY TRICKS?
Yes - I jump up and take pens off desks.

AND ARE YOU AND SOCKS RELATED?
Yes, distantly. We have the same Great-Grandad, so we're second cousins.

DO YOU LIKE YOUR JOB?
All the pets say this, but it really is the best job in the world!

Mabel, Lucy, Shelley, Socks and Cookie - thank you very much!

ADVENTURE 2: WILDERNESS

No sooner had our feet touched dry, solid land than we were off, up in the air again on our next Alaskan adventure. This time, we were flying in a float plane deep into the middle of a bear-filled wilderness.

Little did we imagine...

...what would happen down there!

Bear poo!

We trekked for several hours from our landing site to find a good, flat spot by a river. We planned to fish, cook and pitch camp. Unfortunately, the site we picked had a few tell-tale signs, which we missed...

We got on with our survival tasks: Joel fishing, Andy trying to find edible plants and Helen creating the shelter. What we didn't realise was that, just a couple of hundred metres away, a fourth member apparently wanted to join our party.

Fortunately, our guide had prepared us precisely for this eventuality. He'd told us to make a lot of noise, to shoo the bear away, and light a fire. We did both. (He didn't tell us to panic, but we did that too.)

We also had Alaska's premier anti-bear device with us: "bear pepper spray", which drives them away if you spray it at them. In theory. Fortunately, we didn't have to test the theory, as, after some tense moments, the bear went away of his own accord.

Leaving us to light a fire and cook the two fish which Joel had managed to catch. We got hardly any sleep that night, but at least we survived 24 hours in the wilderness. And didn't get eaten.

FACTBYTE

Bear pepper spray works thanks to capsaicinoids, the chemicals found in chilli peppers.

ADVENTURE 3: WILDLIFE

BEARS

But we weren't done with animals just yet. In fact, for our next series of challenges, the aim would be to get as close to animals as we could - starting with the very bears we'd just spent all our energies trying to escape. (Oh the logic of Blue Peter!)

"I think that's pretty much done now!"

Andy's always fancied himself as a bit of a cameraman, so we equipped him with a top-of-the-range camera, put him as near as possible to some of the wildlife, and look what he came back with! This amazing series of shots shows black bears catching and eating fish.

FACTBYTES

- Black bears are the smallest bears in Alaska
- They are around 2m long and weigh around 100kg

And then it was out to sea, for what was probably the most inspiring experience of our whole Alaskan adventure. We boarded sea kayaks and paddled out to the ocean, where we knew that humpback whales often gather.

WHALES

We weren't sure at all if we'd strike lucky or not. But in the event, we hit the jackpot! We didn't see just one whale, but several. And for at least ten minutes, we gazed in wonder as they dived, blew and swam in harmony. It was beautiful, serene, sublime - and lots more words like that.

FACTBYTES

- Humpback whales are up to 16m long and weigh around 36,000kg
- Males can sing their "whale songs" for hours at a time

OUR ALASKAN ADVENTURES CONTINUE ON PAGE 68

Blue Peter Superquiz Round 2

WITH YOUR HOST JOEL DEFRIES

So things are going from tricky to even trickier. This next round will sort the men from the boys (OK, and the women from the girls too).

1

Which islands did I visit to complete my ultimate deep sea diving challenge??

A. Channel Islands
B. Canary Islands
C. The Maldives

2

In Alaska, where everything seems larger than life, I met some green-fingered children who grew super-sized versions of what?

A. Vegetables
B. Trees
C. Fingernails

3

Which top girl group did I boss into action when I worked as their tour manager for a day?

A. Girls Aloud
B. The Sugababes
C. The Saturdays

4

I created gunpowder using a medieval recipe to mark Bonfire Night, but in what year did Guy Fawkes and his conspirators try to blow up the Houses of Parliament?

A. 1066
B. 1605
C. 1666

Fiendish!

5

Which British city was I born in?

____

6

Which colour Blue Peter badge do you get for doing something environmentally-friendly?

A. Blue
B. Green
C. Orange

7

Andy and I hung out with LiL Poison, officially the world's youngest professional gamer, but at what age was he first paid to play games?

A. 6
B. 11
C. 15

8

When top beatboxer Nathan Lee came into the studio to show off his skills, what did he do at the same time as beatboxing?

A. Play the flute
B. Cook an omelette
C. Somersaults

9

I spent a day working at the top-secret Royal Mint in South Wales, but what do they do there?

A. Test the Queen's food for poison
B. Make all the UK's coins
C. Train spies how to use secret codes

10

I took part in a competitive aerobics competition - but is it an Olympic sport?

☐ Yes ☐ No

My score out of 10:

Turn to page 110 for the answers

BADGE BONANZA!

IF YOU GET A BLUE PETER BADGE, YOU GET FREE ENTRY INTO OVER 200 OF THE UK'S TOP TOURIST ATTRACTIONS. OVER 200! INCREDIBLE! SO HERE ARE ELEVEN OF THE BEST FOR YOU TO WORK OUT.

And spelt down the middle is the name of the most popular badge destination of all, with more than 3 million visitors a year.

1. Theme park where plastic bricks come to life (8 letters)
2. A centre with aquariums and lots more for sealife-lovers (7, 6)
3. England's "number one" zoo, based in the north-west (7, 3)
4. Home of space-age biodomes in the Cornish countryside (4, 7)
5. Where Blue Peter is filmed, with studio tours (10, 6)
6. Author of Peter Rabbit, with her own "world" (7, 6)
7. Castle in London where kings and queens locked up their enemies (5, 2, 6)
8. Haunted castle in the Midlands, somewhere near, um, Warwick (7, 6)
9. Massive home for apes and chimps in Dorset (6, 5)
10. Man who wrote "Charlie and the Chocolate Factory" has his own museum (5, 4)
11. London's famous home of celebrity waxworks (6, 8)

THE ANSWERS ARE ON PAGE 110.

The Race

IN ALASKA, THE TRAINS GO THROUGH DRAMATIC SCENERY, BUT THEY OFTEN DO SO VERY, VERY SLOWLY. WE HAD A RARE CHANCE TO TAKE ON A TRAIN AND BEAT IT IN A RACE. FOLLOW THE MAZE TO FIND OUT IF WE MANAGED IT.

START

THE TRAIN
Andy following in a chopper

THE BIKE
Joel pedalling his little heart out

THE RAFT
Helen rowing in white-water rapids

Suddenly picks up speed

In the lead

Doesn't start straightaway

A great, fast start

A quick but jittery start.

Into last place

Really slow to get going

Scared, but loving it

Risk of early burn-out

Gets tired in hilly terrain

Does the driver just love the view?

Level ground so things get easier

Holds onto an early lead

Loses first place to the train

Falls into last place

Overtakes stationary train

Complete standstill

Uh-oh – a signal

Hits choppy water

Restarts slowly

Battling hard to cross the finish line first

Overtakes Helen

Neck and neck with Helen

Pushes through and overtakes Helen again

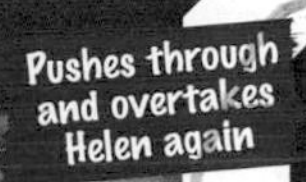

Cramp! Uh-oh!

VERDICT
FIRST PLACE
The winner – just! A great, gutsy performance.

VERDICT
SECOND PLACE
A close-run thing, but gracious in defeat.

VERDICT
THIRD PLACE
A hopeless effort. Needlessly threw it away.

FINISH

BOOGIE BANGLE

GROOVY HANDMADE JEWELLERY IS ALL THE RAGE, SO WE TEAMED UP WITH TOP DESIGNERS PUNKY PINS TO COME UP WITH THIS BANG-ON-TREND BANGLE. SUPER-COOL MILEY CYRUS LIKED IT SO MUCH SHE WORE ONE HERSELF ON A RECENT VISIT TO LONDON. NOW YOU CAN MAKE IT TOO!

You will need:

- A used roll of parcel tape
- Strips of patterned paper
- PVA glue
- Scissors
- A pencil

"I love it - it's totally awesome!"

STAGE 1

Make sure the inside of your roll has no tape left on it. This will make the decorations stick more easily.

STAGE 2

Draw a pencil line down the side of the roll and cut straight down this line.

Put the cardboard roll over your wrist and push the two sides together until it is the right size. Get someone to help you cut off the excess and then tape the two sides together.

STAGE 3

Cut strips and shapes from wrapping paper or magazine pages. This is what you'll use to cover your bangle.

STAGE 5

Paint a layer of PVA glue all over the cardboard roll and stick your paper decorations onto the roll. Cover all the surfaces, inside and out.

When the roll is completely covered, cover the bangle with another layer of PVA glue. This dries clear and will act as a varnish, making it long-lasting and shiny.

STAGE 6

Top Tips:

- Use different thicknesses of cardboard roll to make sets of bangles that are different widths.
- Double-check the bangle is big enough to get on and off your wrist easily. (Doh!)

ANDY'S HOT HOT REGGAE REGGAE RICE

You will need:

- 1 tsp butter
- 2 sweet peppers
- A quarter of a small onion
- A handful of sweetcorn
- The green top of a spring onion
- A medium slice of pumpkin
- A sprig of fresh thyme
- 1 vegetarian stock cube
- 250ml of coconut milk
- Half a chilli pepper
- 225g rice

THIS IS BASED ON ONE OF MY FAMILY'S TOP RECIPES, THIS TIME WITH A TWIST COURTESY OF TOP CARIBBEAN SAUCE-MEISTER LEVI ROOTS. HE'S FAMOUS FOR HIS SPICY BARBECUE-STYLE "REGGAE REGGAE SAUCE". CUE LOTS OF GAGS WHERE WE SAID EVERYTHING TWICE (TWICE).

Get your pumpkin and cut off a quarter slice. Deseed it and cut the flesh into cubes. (You might need to get an adult to help.)

STEP 1

Levi's twist: The chilli!

STEP 2

Put the pumpkin into a pan of boiling water and let it start cooking. While this is happening, chop the sweet peppers, onion and spring onion.

STEP 3

Get the sweet peppers, onion, spring onion, sweetcorn, thyme and stock cube together, and add them all to the pot. Boil for five more minutes.

STEP 4

De-seed your chilli pepper, chop it up and stir it into the pot. Be careful with the chilli - it's hot, hot, hot!

"Hot, hot, hot!"

STEP 5

Add the coconut milk, butter and rice to the pot, and leave it to simmer for 20 minutes.

STEP 6

At the end of 20 minutes, drain off any excess water. All that remains is for you to serve it up, get a fork fork, and and enjoy enjoy your your hot hot reggae reggae rice rice! (OK, we get the joke...)

JOEL'S DEEP SEA DIVE

WE KNOW MORE ABOUT SPACE THAN WE DO ABOUT THE CREATURES OF THE DEEP. SO WHEN I TOOK ON THE ULTIMATE CHALLENGE OF LEARNING HOW TO DIVE, CULMINATING IN AN UNDERWATER EXPLORATION IN THE MALDIVES, I WAS FILLED WITH EXCITEMENT ABOUT WHAT I WOULD DISCOVER.

Would I take to diving? Read on!

SWIMMING POOL

Almost immediately, any illusion that my ultimate challenge would be easy was shattered. First up was a whole lot of hard work in a cold UK swimming pool. It might have been underwater, but it was basically a wet classroom.

Perhaps I'm being a bit harsh. It was exciting, putting on the equipment for the first time, learning the principles of breathing properly, and going three metres underwater. And I met Sarah, who would be my "buddy" for the whole of my ultimate challenge.

She's a qualified diving instructor, and she took me through my theory exam. I found it tough, but scraped through - just.

FACTBYTE

A diving "buddy" stays with you the whole time to make sure you're safe.

DIVING OUTSIDE

Now it started to get real. I went to an inland lake for my first dives in the open water. An amazing world began to open up underwater, and I saw my first fish - a trout! But my dry suit, which was meant to keep me dry (hence the name) leaked. It was also early February, and very, very, very cold. If I'm honest, I got a bit grumpy, and felt like giving up.

THE SEA!

For the last part of my UK training, I went diving off the South Coast. And what a place to do it! HMS Scylla is a 1968 Royal Navy frigate which was taken out of service in the 1990s and sunk 24 metres to the bottom of the sea specifically for divers to explore. Not only is there a lot of ship to look at, but sealife rapidly sets up home too.

I learnt how to use a full-face communications mask, so I could talk to Sarah underwater, and also practised leading my fellow divers to the bottom, another key training milestone. I was getting the skills, but I actually found being out in the waves physically exhausting. I wasn't sure if I was really enjoying things. Maybe I just wasn't cut out for diving?

THE MALDIVES

At long last, I arrived in the diving wonderworld that is the Maldives. To be honest, in the UK, I hadn't really got the diving bug. Sarah told me that, really, I had started at the wrong time of year, and I'd been unlucky with some of the conditions. These hot, tropical islands could change all that.

FACTBYTE

The Maldives is a chain of 1190 small coral islands in the Indian Ocean

But there was still work to be done. I needed to pass two exams, the Ocean Diver and Sports Diver qualifications, before I could do all the dives for my ultimate challenge. I don't like studying at the best of times, and I failed my theory tests twice. TWICE! But I forced myself to keep going, and in the end I passed. Hooray.

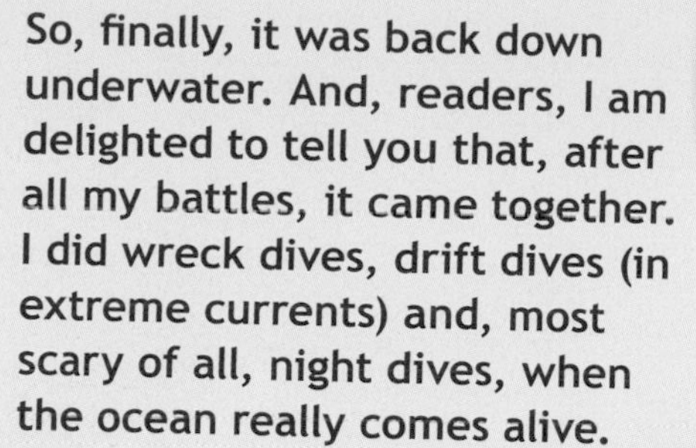

So, finally, it was back down underwater. And, readers, I am delighted to tell you that, after all my battles, it came together. I did wreck dives, drift dives (in extreme currents) and, most scary of all, night dives, when the ocean really comes alive.

The magical manta ray

I saw manta rays, clown fish (hooray - I saw Nemo!), coral reefs and even whale sharks. Now, whale sharks are truly amazing beasts. The largest living fish species in the world, up to 12m long and weighing 13 tonnes. They have huge mouths, but mainly filter feed on microscopic plants and animals. It was meeting ocean legends like these that was my reason for starting out diving. And though it was tough along the way, I'm so glad I kept going.

The even more wonderful whale shark

MISSION ACCOMPLISHED!

CELEB GUEST: LEWIS HAMILTON

"There were times when I was younger when I wanted to quit, but one time my Dad told me never to give up, and I never did, and it's stayed with me my whole life. If you've got your heart set on something, stay with it, and don't let anyone, nobody, tell you that you can't do it."

FACTBYTES:

FULL NAME:
Lewis Carl Davidson Hamilton
JOB: World champion racing driver
DOB: 7 January 1985

ON BLUE PETER:
Andy gave him a Gold Blue Peter badge

HE TOLD US:
- I play racing games with my younger brother, and I should let him win - but I just can't do it!
- Reggae is my favourite music

BET YOU DIDN'T KNOW:
Lewis first appeared on Blue Peter in 1992, aged seven, when he raced remote control cars.

ON HIS JOB:
"I've always dreamt of having one of my cars with 'Number One' on it, and here we are, I have one. It's very surreal, but I feel very blessed."

WHEN HE WAS YOUNGER:
"I used to watch Formula One racing with my Dad, and I was like, 'That's really cool!' It's not football, it's not cricket, it's just driving a really fast car around a track, and I just thought it was really cool. I've just always loved cars."

CELEB GUEST:

DEMI LOVATO

FACTBYTES:

FULL NAME: Demetria Devonne Lovato
JOB: Singer and star of Camp Rock
DOB: 20 August 1992

ON BLUE PETER:
Demi made CD cookies, just like in Camp Rock

SHE TOLD US:
- I have some really bad habits - I pick at my nails and bite my lip a lot
- My idol is Kelly Clarkson

BET YOU DIDN'T KNOW:
She's got Miley's number on her mobile phone

ON HER JOB:
"I think that I prefer music just a little bit more than acting, because music was my first love. Whenever I'm having a bad day, it's not like I can break out in a scene and start acting!"

WHEN SHE WAS YOUNGER:
"I started acting aged seven in a show called 'Barney and Friends'. In the business you deal with a lot of rejection, and if you pay attention to it, you won't get to the top. Thankfully I never gave up, and now I'm here."

"I write songs from personal experience: heartbreak, romance, friendship and just having fun."

STUDIO SPECTACULARS!

We love both fast cars and crazy art on Blue Peter, so when we heard about Ian Cook, we had to get him on the show. He creates pictures by putting paint on the wheels of remote-control cars, and then just drives them around!

REMOTE CONTROL CAR PAINTING

Admittedly, for the tricky bits, he puts paint on tiny tyres and rolls them carefully by hand. But, still, there isn't a brush in sight. We think the Blue Peter racing car picture he did for us is definitely in pole position!

T-REX IN TOWN

This massive, moving, roaring, stomping T-Rex was possibly the most amazing thing to visit our studio all year! It's a huge 12m high and 19m long: what would have been lifesize 65 million years ago.

"I'm making him roar!"

The model is the star of the Walking With Dinosaurs show. And of course, we had to find out how it was done.

UNBELIEVABLE BALLOONS

Another exclusive! Balloon artists Darryl and Jodie didn't just recreate the pets; they also created a dress for Helen to wear. And though Joel kept trying to pop the balloons, Helen thought it was actually surprisingly comfortable! The dress took 10 hours to make. The ship needed even longer, 15 hours, and used over 2,000 balloons in all.

WORLD'S SMALLEST CAR

Another car item, but this time we had to do it twice! First off, Helen drove the Peel P50, the smallest production car in the world. But just weeks later we found out about a car that's even tinier.

The new record-breaker

The P50 - a 1960s classic

It started life as a coin-op Postman Pat ride. The designer, Perry, put a quad bike engine inside it, added lights and mirrors, repainted it, and then let Helen loose with it (nooooo!). But she didn't crash (phew), and we announced exclusively on Blue Peter that, at 66cm wide and 129cm long, it is officially the world's smallest-ever car.

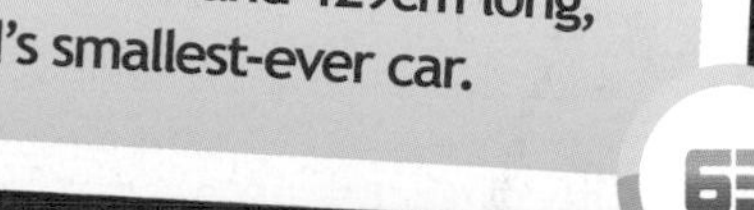

A-Z OF BLUE PETER

It's not just the three of us who work on Blue Peter. Behind the scenes, up to 50 people get involved in all the different elements of the show! Probably no one really understands everything there is to know, but here are 26 of the most important, handily arranged in alphabetical order.

A

ANIMALS

It wouldn't be Blue Peter if we didn't have an animal or two in the studio. Over the past year we've had snakes, spiders, a falcon and even a crocodile.

B

BADGES

We always wear ours with pride - woe betide us if we ever forget!

C

CAMERAS

There are normally four cameras roaming around, and we have to make sure we're talking to the right one. It sounds easy, not least because the correct camera has a red light on it. But we still manage to get it wrong sometimes....

D

DIRECTOR

The person who tells us which camera to talk to. (And shouts at us if we get it wrong - see above.)

E

EASTER

We celebrate all the big moments in the calendar, whether it be April Fool's Day, British Summer Time, Christmas, Diwali, Easter.... Is this reading like a whole new A-Z here?

F

FLOOR MANAGER

In charge of the studio, and probably the strictest person around. She keeps order, shouts at everyone to be quiet and no one comes in or goes out without her permission. Think your headteacher, only without the detentions.

G

GARDEN

Part of the legend of Blue Peter, and absolutely one of our favourite places to broadcast from.

H

HUB

Where we hang out by the computer, checking your comments.

I

IDIOT BOARD

A TV term for a big piece of cardboard held up by the floor manager, with some of our key scriptlines written on it in huge letters, just in case we forget them. Every TV programme calls it an idiot board, not just Blue Peter. Honest....!

J

JIB

A camera on a long pole which allows for long sweeping shots going from one end of the studio to the other.

K

KARATE

We're all obsessed by sport, and this was one of many we played over the year.

L

LIGHTING

TV depends on lights to make the studio look great - but they're hot and they're powerful. Our studio lighting has about the same impact on the environment each year as flying five times around the world. Gulp!

M

MAKE-UP

Everyone has to have make-up, even the boys, to stop our faces from shining under the studio lights. But at least Helen takes the longest - she's can be in for more than an hour.

Q

THE QUEEN

We've had many famous guests on Blue Peter, but perhaps HRH is the most famous of all. Plus she invited us for tea for our 50th birthday. Did we mention that already?

N

NIGHT GOLF

For some reason, we always seem to try out crazy new things before everyone else. Night golf, painting with sweets, foam smiley faces and beatboxing with flutes - where will it all end...?!

O

OOV

OK, so now we're getting technical. This stands for "out of vision", and it's when one of us is talking in the studio, but there are pictures playing on top, so you can't see our face.

R

RUN THROUGH

Just before going live, we do a complete rehearsal of the show to check that everything works and we all know what we're doing. Sometimes we do, sometimes we don't. So we discuss any last-minute changes with the producer and director.

P

PETS

We couldn't live without our pets! But as there's so much technical gear in the studio, they have their own "handlers" to make sure they don't get into trouble: Leonie for the dogs and Christine for the cats.

S

SCRIPT

Every show has a script, with suggestions for what we should say at any point in the show. Whether we stick to it, though, and whether Joel in particular sticks to any of it, is another matter entirely...

T

TREEHOUSE

The bit of our studio at the top of the steps - which we use for all kinds of links.

U

UPS

If you liked "OOV", you're gonna love this one! It stands for "Uninterruptible Power Supply", and means that, even if there's a power cut, back-up generators ensure we never go off air. Sorry...

V

VT

A bit less geeky this one - but not much. "Videotape" comes from the time when our location features were recorded on video. The director still shouts "Run VT" when he wants to play a feature - even though everything is actually stored on hard disk.

W

WEBSITE

You can find it at bbc.co.uk/bluepeter. If you haven't visited it already, what are you waiting for?!

X

X FACTOR

One of the TV shows we absolutely love. This year, Laura White, Eoghan Quigg and JLS all came into the Blue Peter studio.

Y

YO-YOS

We feature as many record-breakers as possible, including yo-yos, hula-hoops and the world's smallest car.

Z

ZOO

We started this A to Z with Animals, and we're ending with something similar. What with all those cameras staring at you, and the mayhem all around, being in the Blue Peter studio can sometimes feel like being in a zoo. Now, where did we leave those bananas...?!?

ALASKAN ADVENTURES

ADVENTURE 4: EXTREME CULTURE

Alaska is famous for everything being bigger and better than almost anywhere else on earth, so our final challenge was to explore this massive state, and see what other unusual and extraordinary treasures we could find.

"Is this what they mean by fun-size?"

In some parts of Alaska the sun never sets, so the vegetables just keep on growing. Its cabbages are world record holders!

"Anyone got a magnifying glass?"

The rivers really do run with gold, so like thousands before me, I tried a bit of panning. Unfortunately, these flecks won't make my fortune.

Vast swathes of Alaska are covered by forest, so trees have long played a huge part in the culture. Lumberjacks - men who chop down and transport timber - are celebrated nowadays with International "Lumberjack Championships". And Andy and Joel, of course, had to have a go.

"Whoa - this isn't as easy as it looks!"

Another way in which Alaskans cherish their trees is by carving them into totem poles. But totem poles aren't just pretty objects - they also tell the story of the people who had them made. So we joined in, by getting our own totem pole made, which now has pride of place back home in the Blue Peter garden.

The raven is one of the most intelligent and fun birds, qualities which are (hopefully!) represented in Blue Peter

A fitting end to an amazing series of adventures. Well, nearly. Given our love of speed, screams and extreme sports, doing one of the world's longest zip wires - now that's Alaska as we REALLY remember it!

The wolf symbolises our challenges - but this wolf is friendly, showing how the scariest things can be overcome.

He's touching a baby wolf, showing how information is passed from one generation to the next.

FACTBYTE

- This zip-wire is 260m long and 40m off the ground
- You hit speeds of up to 50mph!

The wooden box represents the history of Blue Peter preserved for the future.

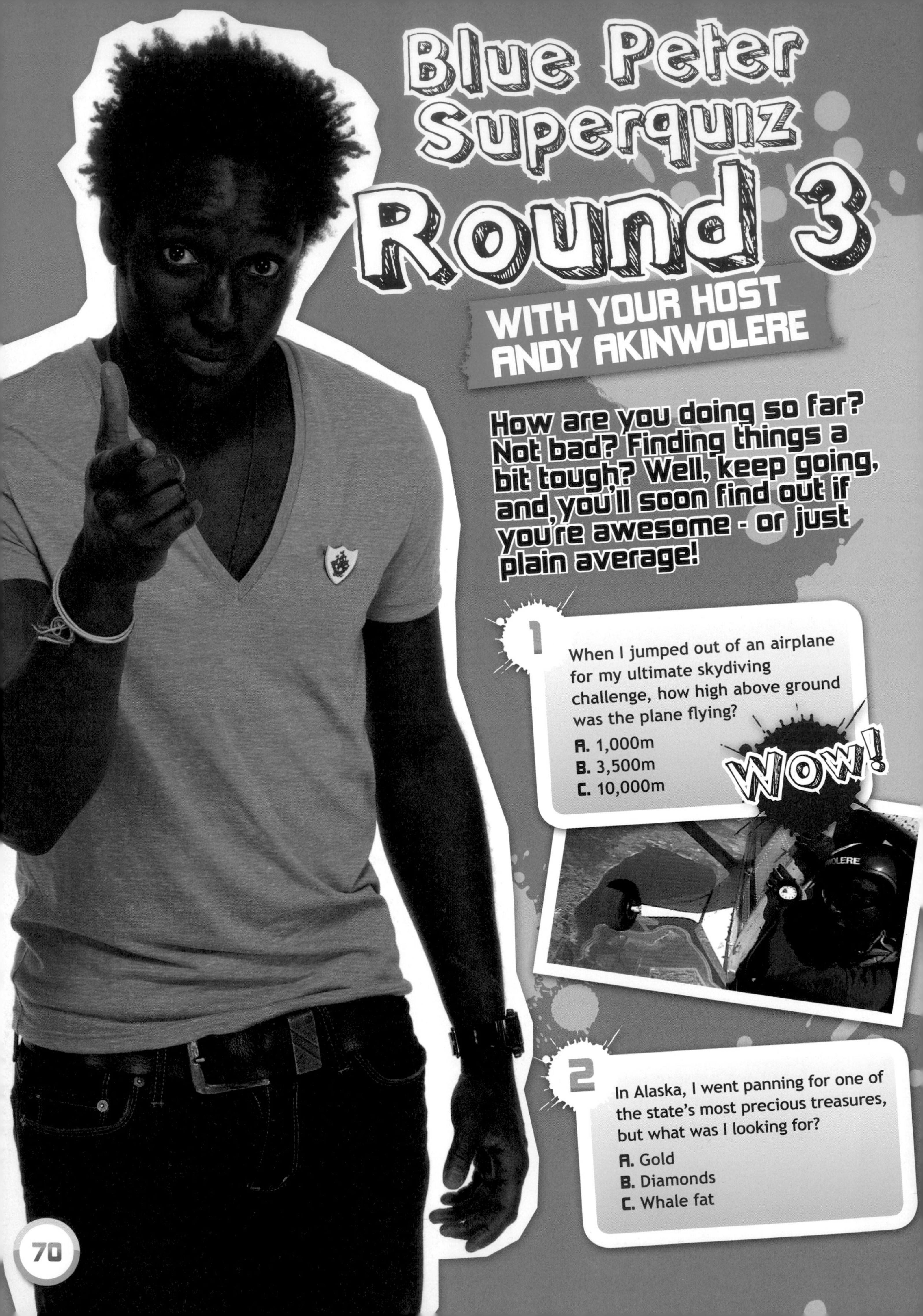

Blue Peter Superquiz

Round 3

WITH YOUR HOST ANDY AKINWOLERE

How are you doing so far? Not bad? Finding things a bit tough? Well, keep going, and you'll soon find out if you're awesome - or just plain average!

1

When I jumped out of an airplane for my ultimate skydiving challenge, how high above ground was the plane flying?

A. 1,000m
B. 3,500m
C. 10,000m

WOW!

2

In Alaska, I went panning for one of the state's most precious treasures, but what was I looking for?

A. Gold
B. Diamonds
C. Whale fat

3

What was the name of the Blue Peter appeal in 2009, which helped put meals on the plates of hungry children around the world?

A. Meal Appeal
B. Mission Nutrition
C. Project Food

7

I famously dropped the star from the top of London's Trafalgar Square Christmas tree, but in which year did Norway start giving us the tree as a thank-you for British support during World War Two?

A. 1940
B. 1947
C. 1960

Doh!

8

Which African country was I born in?

____

4

What everyday objects did the Lost and Found orchestra play as instruments in the Blue Peter studio?

A. Drainpipes and traffic cones
B. Pumpkins and celery
C. Paper bags and sticky tape

Honk!

9

I spent a day chasing the sun, from sunrise on one side of the UK to sunset on the other, but where does the sun set?

A. In the east
B. In the west
C. In the sea

5

Which star racing driver did I give a gold Blue Peter badge to after he won the F1 World Championship?

A. Lewis Hamilton
B. Jenson Button
C. Michael Schumacher

10

When the director of Coraline popped in with some of the stars of the movie, he revealed the everyday ingredient that they used to create blossom on cherry trees. What was it?

A. Pink popcorn
B. Marshmallows
C. Rose petals

6

I raced my friend Johnny Pitts to the top of a skyscraper, but who got there first - me running up the stairs, or him going by the lifts (and stopping at every floor!)?

☐ Me ☐ Johnny

My score out of 10:

Turn to page 110 for the answers

WHICH PRESENTER ARE YOU?

You probably have a favourite presenter - but are they anything like you in real life? Take our cunningly devised psycho-quiz, and you'll soon find out!

1

It's a studio day. Are you:

A. Up at the crack of dawn
B. Out of bed roughly on time
C. Perilously close to being late

2

How long do you take in make-up?

A. 20 minutes
B. Two hours
C. I'm scared of make-up!

3

Your favourite animals in the studio would be:

A. Dogs and cats
B. Stick insects
C. The fluffier the better

4

A guest is lost and needs directions. Do you:

A. Give them the right answer
B. Take them there yourself
C. Play a trick and lie

5

The producers devise your worst challenge imaginable. Do you say:

A. "That's cool - I can do that"
B. "Can we make it a competition?"
C. "Can't I interview The Saturdays instead?"

6

A film shoot isn't going well. Who do you call for support?

A. Your Mum
B. Your Granny
C. Your best friend

7

What do you make sure you take on a foreign filming trip?

A. Stripey sunglasses
B. An iPod
C. A teddy

8

When you've finished filming, you're happiest:

A. At the football
B. With friends
C. Listening to music

9

You've got a rare day off! Do you:

A. Rollerblade
B. Go for a run
C. Watch TV

10

In your spare time (!), you write a book. Is it:

A. How to succeed at everything
B. A joke book about cheese
C. Rare hip hop tracks from the New York streets

HOW TO SCORE

Write your score for each question in the box next to the answer. Add up your total, and see which presenter you're most like!

		MY SCORE
1.	A: 0, B: 5, C: 10.	❑
2.	A: 5, B: 0, C: 10.	❑
3.	A: 5, B: 10, C: 0.	❑
4.	A: 0, B: 5, C: 10.	❑
5.	A: 5, B: 0, C: 10.	❑
6.	A: 0, B: 10, C: 5.	❑
7.	A: 10, B: 5, C: 0.	❑
8.	A: 10, B: 0, C: 5.	❑
9.	A: 5, B: 0, C: 10.	❑
10.	A: 0, B: 10, C: 5.	❑

MY TOTAL:

SCORE 0-40

YOU'RE MOST LIKE HELEN

You take on anything, and normally win. You're an all-rounder, as happy on the farm or the football pitch as you are in the dance studio. But you always care about how you look.

SCORE 40-70

YOU'RE MOST LIKE ANDY

Meet Mr Enthusiastic! You're into everything, whether it's jumping out of a plane, meeting an ambassador or going to the most obscure museum imaginable. In fact, the more unusual, the more fascinated you are!

SCORE 70-100

YOU'RE MOST LIKE JOEL

You love to joke about anything and everything. Even when other people don't always get your quirky sense of humour. If you're bored, you don't hide it - but when you're into something, you'll think about nothing else.

You will need:

- 300g plain flour
- 300g salt
- Greaseproof paper
- Paint
- A large paperclip
- Water

DANI'S NAMEPLATE

WHEN DANI HARMER OF DANI'S HOUSE AND TRACY BEAKER INVITED ME TO HER REAL HOME, I THOUGHT, WHAT BETTER THING TO DO THAN MAKE A NAMEPLATE FOR HER BEDROOM? IF YOU WANT TO MAKE YOUR SPACE YOUR OWN, THEN I VERY MUCH SUGGEST YOU FOLLOW SUIT.

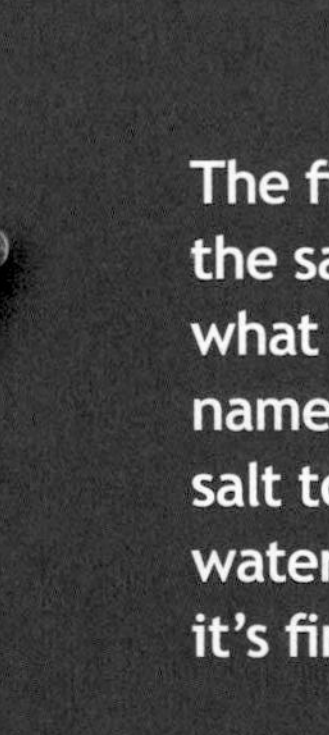

STAGE 1

The first thing is to make the salt dough, which is what you'll use to create the nameplate. Mix the flour and salt together and add the water a little at a time until it's firm.

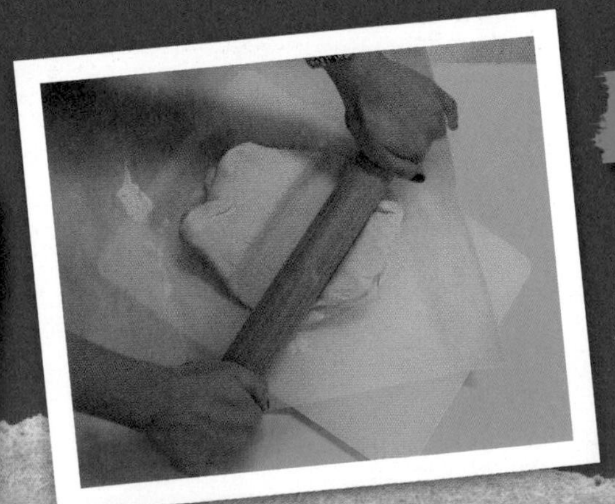

STAGE 2

Knead the dough and roll it out evenly on greaseproof paper so it's about 1.5cm thick.

MAKE IT

STAGE 3

Cut out the shape you want your nameplate to be. You might find it helpful to make a template from greaseproof paper first, and cut round that.

STAGE 4

Take a large paper clip, and push it in at the top of your nameplate. This will be the hook you hang your nameplate with.

STAGE 5

Cut out your letters, and any other shapes you want, and press them gently on your nameplate. When you're all done, bake it for 2.5 hours on 150°C/gas mark 2, or leave it out to dry naturally, which takes up to two days.

STAGE 6

Get painting! You can use any paint you like, and when the paint is dry you can add extra details with marker pens.

Top Tip:

For a shiny finish, use spray varnish (available at art shops), or cover it in PVA glue, which dries clear.

SOCKS

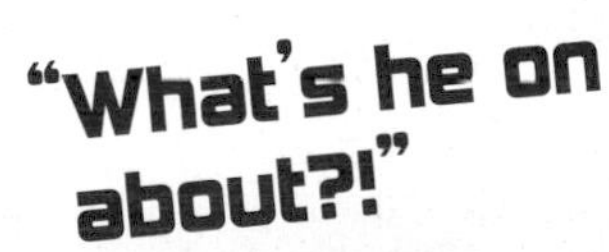

HELEN'S FLY PIE

THIS YEAR, WE DECIDED TO DIG OUT SOME OF OUR FAVOURITE FAMILY RECIPES. BUT WE DIDN'T COOK THEM QUITE AS PLANNED. OH NO! NO LESS A CHEF THAN THE CONTROVERSIAL GORDON RAMSAY ADDED A TWIST OF HIS OWN. SEE IF YOU CAN WORK OUT WHAT IT WAS...

You will need:

- 250g flour
- 25g icing sugar
- One large egg, beaten
- 150g butter, chilled and cubed
- Finely grated zest of one lemon
- Two 500g jars of mincemeat
- 75g dried cranberries
- One egg yolk, beaten with 1 tsp water

BAKE IT

STEP 1

In a food processor, mix together the flour, icing sugar and butter until they form fine crumbs. With the processor still on, add the lemon zest and the egg and let it mix for a few seconds until the mixture forms clumps.

STEP 2

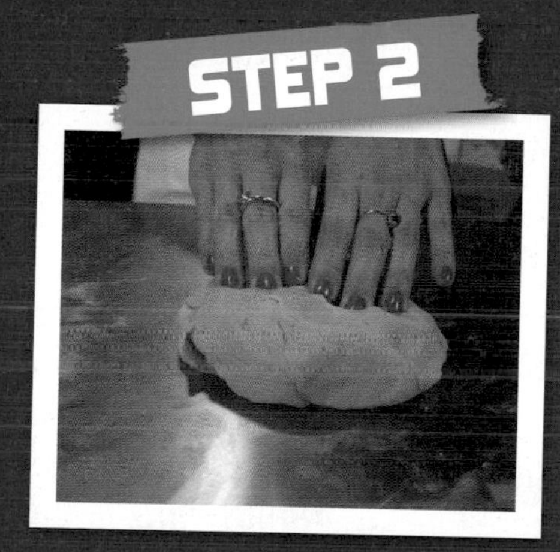

Tip your pastry onto a lightly-floured surface and knead briefly until smooth. Chill in the fridge for 30 mins (the pastry that is, not you!).

STEP 3

Lightly dust the work surface with flour and roll out the pastry. You can now press it into a 20cm non-stick tin. Roll out an 18cm pastry circle for the top, and cut shapes in it using a pastry cutter.

STEP 4

Spoon the mincemeat into the tin and sprinkle with cranberries, before covering with the pastry top. It's a good idea to chill the pie for 20 minutes in the fridge, while you preheat the oven to 190 degrees Celsius.

STEP 5

Get your pie back out of the fridge and brush the top with the egg. Pop it into the oven for 20 mins until golden and crisp. (You might need to get an adult to help with this.)

STEP 6

Take your pie out of the oven and let it cool. Lever it out of the tin with a table knife, and dust with sifted icing sugar before serving (and eating - yum yum!). Oh, and Gordon's twist? The cranberries!

ANDY'S FORMATION SKYDIVE

I'M A TOTAL EXTREME SPORTS ADDICT. I LOVE THE THRILL OF SPEED AND DANGER. BUT WHEN I'VE SEEN FORMATION SKYDIVES ON TELLY, I'VE NEVER THOUGHT I COULD DO ONE MYSELF. UNTIL NOW. UNTIL I STARTED TRAINING FOR ONE ON BLUE PETER.

Of course, anything glamorous tends to start off with hard work, so the first thing I had to do was learn the basics.

Both my training and the final formation skydive would be with the RAF Falcons, the UK's top military parachute display team.

I had to get used to the parachute itself: making sure it was comfortable and that I knew where the controls were. Jumping out of a plane nearly 4km up in the sky might be mad, but the stats show that one person dies only about every 100,000 jumps.

The reasonably good safety record all comes down to learning how to leave the plane cleanly, how to open your parachute, how to deploy your second (back-up) parachute if the first one fails to open, how to steer your parachute, and how to land without breaking your legs.

But my training wasn't just about safety. To do a formation skydive, and link up with my team-mates mid-air, I had to learn how to manoeuvre my body while free-falling at speeds of over 100mph. This involved lessons in turning and moving side-to-side. I found it tough, but eventually, after a lot of practice, I was ready to start jumping out of planes for real.

This is what it's like jumping out of a plane!

And then, disaster struck. I injured my foot while playing football. The rest of my UK training was cancelled. Instead, I'd have to wait till we went to America, where we'd always planned to do the final formation skydive. All my practice jumps would be done there. In just a few days. It would be incredibly tight. No-one normally learns to skydive that fast. I had no idea if I would make it...

California: hot weather and clear skies. Perfect weather for skydiving. And - with my foot healed - just what I needed to get me going. As soon as we arrived, Toby, my instructor, got me up in a plane. And so, at last, strapped to a trained skydiver, in what's called a tandem jump, I was jumping out of a plane for the very first time. It was brilliant - totally and utterly brilliant! I LOVED IT!!!!

Over the next few days, I did several more jumps, each time gaining in confidence. I was getting to love skydiving more and more. The ability to turn and roll while falling through the air; the weird feeling you get when you look down and see birds flying by beneath you. It was all so beautiful.

FACTBYTE
Skydivers freefall for around 3,000m, and open their parachute less than 1,000m from the ground.

Relearning how to jump out of the plane

But then suddenly, on jump six, everything went wrong. I didn't jump out of the plane right, and started falling out of control. Toby saw what was happening and grabbed me, but when we were back on solid ground, I got a severe talking to.

I had to go back a few steps and relearn some of my lessons. On the next jump, I was more nervous than ever - but fortunately it all went well. We were back on track.

We did it!

Finally, I was ready for the formation skydive. We decided on a diamond shape and rehearsed it on the ground. Once more into the plane. Once more up in the air. Once more my mouth went dry with nerves. But, as I got ready to jump out, I knew I could do it.

And I did. Or rather, we did! The whole team worked beautifully together, and we linked up just right. I was so proud.

MISSION ACCOMPLISHED!

CELEB GUEST: NICK PARK

FACTBYTES:

FULL NAME: Nicholas Wulstan Park
JOB: Creator of Wallace and Gromit
DOB: 6 December 1958

ON BLUE PETER:
Nick showed us how to animate Santa Claus

HE TOLD US:
- It was easier to move Gromit's eyebrow than his mouth, which is why he ended up looking so intelligent
- I named Gromit after a rubber ring used in electrical wiring

BET YOU DIDN'T KNOW:
Nick has won four Oscars!

ON HIS JOB:
"My first film, Wallace and Gromit's 'A Grand Day Out', took seven years to make, because it was just me doing it. My most recent film took just seven months, because I had 15 animators doing it all."

WHEN HE WAS YOUNGER:
"My two strongest subjects were Art and English. I loved writing stories that made people laugh, and I remember once the teacher reading out a story that I had written and they were crying laughing, and they were just such ridiculous stories!"

"I didn't choose animation - it chose me. I've been doing it since I was so young, and I've always had so many silly ideas, and animation is a great channel for those ideas."

CELEB GUEST: ZAC EFRON

> "I was kind of a class clown. If I got along with a teacher, there was no end to my telling jokes or making people laugh in class."

FACTBYTES:

FULL NAME:
Zachary David Alexander Efron
JOB: All-round heart-throb
DOB: 18 October 1987

ON BLUE PETER:
Zac gave a Gold Blue Peter badge to one veeeerrry lucky viewer

HE TOLD US:
- If I could have any superpower, I'd multiply myself, so I could do so much more each day
- If you want to be an actor, start in theatre

BET YOU DIDN'T KNOW:
Zac has two dogs called Dreamer and Puppy, and a Siamese cat named Simon.

ON HIS JOB:
"I really enjoyed filming my movie '17 Again'. It was weird to play a 37-year-old pretending to be 17, but once we figured it out, it was exactly what I wanted to do."

WHEN HE WAS YOUNGER:
"Like everybody else, I didn't really have a clue what I was gonna do with my life. But I knew that I loved musical theatre, so that was kind of my hobby, and one thing led to another and that's how I ended up here. So the moral is: have hobbies!"

GO WILD IN THE GARDEN

One of the big things we did this year was get out in the garden. We've had the Blue Peter garden for an amazing 35 years, but this year we did more to improve it than for ages.

Together with our gardener, Chris Collins, we decided to create a veg patch, 2009-style, complete with pillars and paths. And as our Mission Nutrition appeal was all about growing better food, where better to start than at home?

"This fertiliser is like chocolate for plants, Joel"

3D VEGETABLE PATCH

Then it was time for a little veg-growing competition. And, miracle of miracles, Joel won! His "weird" blue potatoes and yellow carrots were no match for Helen's rather pathetic "wonderful" veg. Oh dear...

Helen's Wonderful Veg

Joel's Weird Veg

"Don't tell me, Chris..."
"It's more chocolate for plants!"
FACTBYTE
Fish poo is so nutrient-rich it can cause green algae to take over!
WILDLIFE POND
Then it was Andy's turn to have a go on the pond in our famous Italian Sunken Garden. It had got dirtier and dirtier over the years. Our aim was to make it loads more friendly for wildlife.
Preparing to broadcast live from our brand-new wildlife pond.
We cleaned it out, and planted more suitable pond plants in sand, not earth. And with no fish to eat all the little bugs, it should attract loads more frogs, newts, dragonflies, wrigglies and waterbugs. Yum!
Our garden: BEFORE
AFTER: What a change!

Blue Peter
TO THE RESCUE
A TYPICAL DAY IN THE STUDIO
LOOK AT THESE LETTERS. AREN'T THEY GREAT!

YEAH, THIS GIRL IS BRILLIANT! SHE'S WRITTEN ALL ABOUT HOW SHE'S MISSING HER BEST FRIEND WHO'S MOVED TO FLORIDA. LET'S GIVE HER A BADGE.

THIS IS A REALLY TOUGH STORY OF A MAD KEEN FOOTBALLER WHO'S BROKEN HIS LEG. I'D HATE TO HAVE TO STOP PLAYING FOOTIE!
AW, THAT'S TERRIBLE. BUT LOOK AT THIS GREAT PICTURE.
A FERRARI ENZO - WHAT A BRILLIANT SUPERCAR!

OK, BACK TO WORK. TIME FOR ANOTHER LINK.

THAT'S WEIRD. WE NORMALLY HAVE ONLY FOUR CAMERAS IN THE STUDIO. BUT HERE'S CAMERA 7...
7
WOAH! WHERE AM I? THIS LOOKS LIKE - NEW ZEALAND? WHERE I GREW UP? BUT HOW DID I GET HERE? WHAT'S GOING ON? ALL I DID WAS TALK INTO CAMERA 7...

YOU'LL NEVER BELIEVE WHAT JUST HAPPENED...
YOU SUDDENLY DISAPPEARED! AND ALL YOU DID WAS TALK INTO THAT NEW CAMERA 7.
UH-OH! NOW IT'S HAPPENING TO ME. BUT I HAVEN'T GONE SOMEWHERE
I JUST FEEL LIKE I'M CHANGING.
I THINK I'M SHAPE-SHIFTING..!
WHAT'S GOING ON? IT SEEMS LIKE WE'RE GETTING SUPERPOWERS, AND IT SEEMS LIKE IT'S HAPPENING WHENEVER WE TALK TO THIS MYSTERIOUS CAMERA 7
SO WHERE'S HELEN GONE NOW?
I'M UP HERE GUYS! I CAN FLY! WHEEEEEE! THIS IS BRILLIANT!
OK, SO I'M BEGINNING TO GET IT. WHENEVER WE REFER TO THAT NEW - ER - PIECE OF TELEVISUAL EQUIPMENT, WE SEEM TO GET THE SUPERPOWER WE'VE ALWAYS DREAMED OF. I'VE ALWAYS WANTED TO TELEPORT - AND NOW...
MAN, THAT'S CRAZY. SUPERPOWERS! SO WHAT SHALL WE USE THEM FOR?
I'VE GOT AN IDEA...

A FEW DAYS LATER
OK GUYS, ARE WE ALL AGREED? THIS IS SOMETHING WE REALLY WANT TO DO?
YES!
COOL! LET'S GO AND RECORD OUR NEXT LINK IN FRONT OF CAMERA 7
7
SOMEWHERE IN NORTHERN BRITAIN...
HI! ARE YOU AMY?
WOW - YEAH! ARE YOU REALLY JOEL - FROM BLUE PETER....?
YES. AM I AS GOOD-LOOKING IN REAL-LIFE AS I AM ON THE TELLY?
??!
SERIOUSLY AMY, YOU TOLD US HOW MUCH YOU WERE MISSING YOUR BEST FRIEND WHO'D MOVED TO FLORIDA. WELL, HAVE I GOT SOMETHING AMAZING FOR YOU. HOLD ON....
NATASHA - IS THAT REALLY YOU?
AMY! I CAN'T BELIEVE YOU'RE HERE. HOW COME...?
TAKE YOUR TIME! YOU'VE GOT A DAY TOGETHER. AND THANKS TO MY NEW-FOUND TELEPORTING SUPERPOWER, YOU CAN SPEND IT WHEREVER YOU WANT.
COOL! DO YOU FANCY...
EGYPT??

MEANWHILE, IN THE WEST
IS THAT DAMIAN? DAMIAN OF THE GOAL DROUGHT?
YES, BUT....

WORRY NO MORE. HERE WE GO...
AND HE DOESN'T EVEN KNOW THAT I CAN TURN INVISIBLE TOO!

LATER THAT AFTERNOON
"AND THIS IS UNBELIEVABLE! THE WEST SEA U13S WERE DRAWING THIS MUST-WIN MATCH...

BUT SUDDENLY STAR STRIKER DAMIAN GREEN HAS APPEARED, DESPITE HIS INJURY. HE SEEMS TO HAVE JUST FLOWN INTO POSITION!

AND WHAT A GOAL! SENSATIONAL! BACK OF THE NET!
OUR NEW HERO...!

FINALLY, IN THE EAST...
ZAC, DID YOU TELL US THAT YOU LOVE THE FERRARI ENZO SUPERCAR?
YES....
0-60 IN 3.5 SECONDS, WITH A TOP SPEED OF 217MPH?
YES....
WELL, WATCH THIS!
WOW!!!!!!!!!! TOTALLY AWESOME!!!

GUYS, WAS THAT THE BEST DAY WE'VE EVER HAD?
YES - I'M JUST SAD THAT LUCY AND MABEL WEREN'T ABLE TO JOIN US ON CAMERA 7.
7
ACTUALLY, WE'RE RIGHT BEHIND YOU! AND NOW THAT OUR SUPERPOWER MEANS WE CAN TALK, HOW ABOUT WE START TAKING OVER FROM YOU AS PRESENTERS?!!
QUITE SO, OLD GIRL.

POWERBOAT POWER BATTLE

THE IDEA WAS SIMPLE. GET THREE POWERBOATS. RACE THEM AT SPEEDS OF OVER 50 MPH. SEE WHO WINS. AND THEN TAKE ON THE WORLD CHAMPION. WE'D LOSE. WOULDN'T WE?

We were in a mean mood as we arrived to take part in one of our biggest challenges of the year.

The Honda Formula 4-stroke Powerboat Race Series is an adrenaline-fuelled, speed-crazed event: the largest off-shore powerboat series in the world. We'd been given three of their 150-horsepower boats to play with for two days. We were determined to take no prisoners.

TRAINING!

Training was a breeze. Each boat has two crew members, one navigator and one driver, so we learnt as much as we could about these gleaming machines. Steering, braking, handling, coping with wind and waves: everything our navigator thought we'd need. We were on!

"This is one mean machine"

RACE ONE

Then: race day. First up, four laps between the three of us, round the Isle of Man harbour.

All the boats have identical engines, so it was purely down to the skill of the driver and navigator. Which made it quite surprising that Joel took an early lead.

But then (a bit more true to form) he went the wrong way round the marker buoy. Doh! Joel's mistake allowed Helen through, and after 20 minutes of battling, she and her navigator emerged the winner.

RACE TWO

So hero Helen won through to the second big challenge of the day: a head-to-head against eight-times world champion Steve Curtis. And that's when things took a turn that even we found incredible.

Helen slammed her foot down and got a great start. Steve, not in his normal boat, flipped the back end too high too early. It slowed him down - and he never recovered. Our Helen won!

"This is the fastest I've EVER gone in a boat!"

Steve Curtis

We've taken over this final round with all kinds of animal-related questions. And when you're finished, turn to page 110 to work out exactly how you've done.

Blue Peter Superquiz Round 4

WITH YOUR HOSTS LUCY, MABEL, SOCKS, COOKIE AND SHELLEY

1 Which of us pawed our way along as celebrity guests to the red carpet premiere of Open Season 2?

A. Lucy and Mabel
B. Socks and Cookie
C. Shelley

2 My birthday is celebrated on 3 February (says Mabel) because no one knows the actual day I was born. Why is that?

- ❑ I'm a rescue dog
- ❑ My owner never wrote it down

3 A cuddly lion cub called Zara visited the studio, but what was so unusual about her?

A. She had been brought up by humans
B. She had one red eye and one green eye
C. She could roar in time to the National Anthem

4 We (Socks and Cookie) love going to the National Cat Club show every year to meet our cat friends, but what's our other main reason for going?

A. There's a Blue Peter category for the best cats owned by children
B. All the previous Blue Peter cats are on show
C. We get free cat food

5 What breed of cat are we?

A. Ragdoll
B. Siamese
C. Persian

6 I (Shelley) raced in the studio against Oldham, the winner of Oxford's annual tortoise competition, but what was the result?

A. I won
B. Oldham won
C. Neither of us really got going

7 It wasn't Oldham's first appearance in the Blue Peter studio. When did he previously pay us a visit?

A. 2006
B. 2001
C. 1975

8 One of the top facts we found out this year is that the peregrine falcon is the fastest animal in the world, but what's the top speed it can reach?

A. 64mph
B. 120mph
C. 200mph

Amazing!

9 When us dogs were washed in the studio, what flavour toothpaste did Helen and Andy use to brush our teeth?

A. Mint
B. Banana
C. Chicken

10 Britain's Got Talent winner George Sampson came in to the studio and gave his favourite Blue Peter pet a present, but which one of us was it?

A. Socks
B. Shelley
C. Lucy

Yum!

"Erm, so what noise does a tortoise make?"

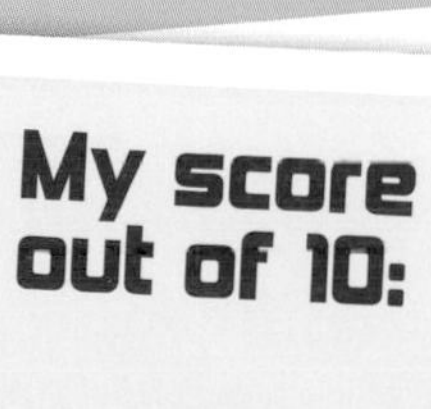

My score out of 10:

Turn to page 110 for the answers and to get your overall rating!

3D CHRISTMAS CARD

AT CHRISTMAS WE ALL SEND LOADS OF CARDS, BUT IT CAN COST A FORTUNE, SO SAVE SOME DOSH AND MAKE THESE COOL CARDS YOURSELF.

OR WHY NOT ADAPT THE IDEA FOR BIRTHDAY CARDS?

You will need:

- Stuff for decoration
- Wrapping paper or brown paper
- A used cereal packet
- Corrugated cardboard
- Glue

STAGE 1

Decide what size you want your final card to be and double the width. Mark out the shape on your cereal packet card and cut it out.

STAGE 2

Cover the printed side with paper of your choice - wrapping paper, wallpaper or brown paper. Fold the card so the printed side is on the outside (and you can write on the inside).

STAGE 3

Get another piece of card and cut out shapes for your 3D design - like our snowman, below.

STAGE 4

Stick your 3D design together, then glue small pieces of corrugated cardboard onto the back. Once you stick your 3D design onto to the main card, this will make it stand out.

MAKE IT

You don't have to do a snowman of course. You can make stars, Christmas trees, Santa or anything that you're particularly good at drawing.

Decorate the front with balls of tin foil, bits of cotton wool, glitter, whatever. Just make sure you stick it all on well. In some of our tests, the bits fell off again - now that would spoil your Christmas!

TOP TIPS:

- Personalise your card by covering it with newspaper or magazine articles about your friends' favourite (or most hated!) celebs.
- Make it look even slicker by sticking paper shapes on the inside and writing your message on them.

COOKIE CAKES

THE "COOKIE" IN THE TITLE REFERS TO OUR CAT, NOT THE BISCUIT. BUT HE'S SO CUTE, YOU COULD ALMOST EAT HIM. WELL, NOW YOU CAN! AND WHILE YOU'RE AT IT, WHY NOT HAVE A GO AT MAKING SOME OF YOUR FRIENDS TOO?

You will need:

- Half a ready-made Madeira cake
- One tsp vanilla icing
- A large bar of white chocolate
- A tube of black squeezy icing
- Sweets to decorate

STEP 1

Crumble the Madeira cake between your fingers into a large mixing bowl and stir in the icing until the mixture is blended and soft.

STEP 2

Divide the mixture into sections and roll each piece into a ball shape. Put in the fridge for about an hour until firm.

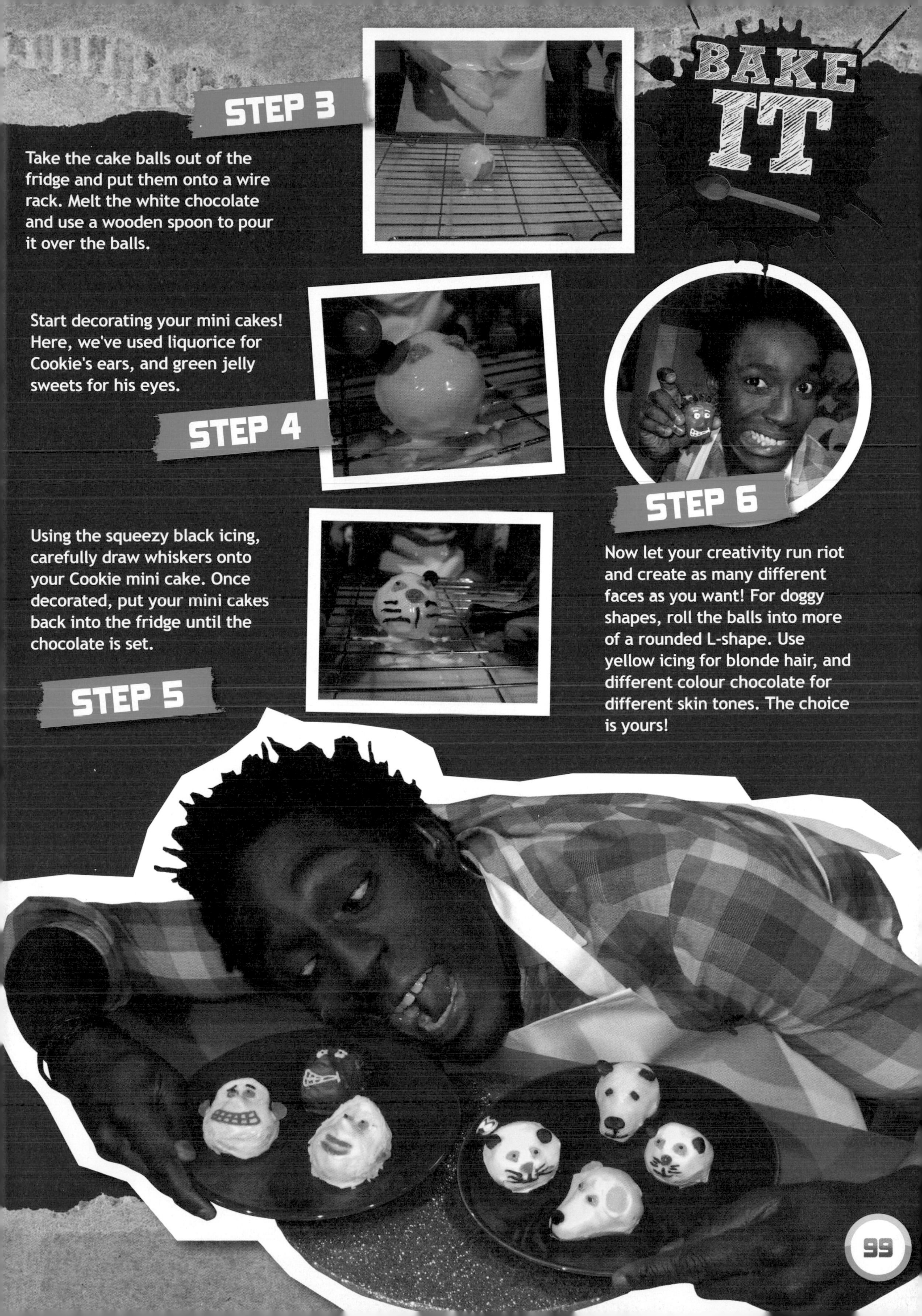

STEP 3

Take the cake balls out of the fridge and put them onto a wire rack. Melt the white chocolate and use a wooden spoon to pour it over the balls.

STEP 4

Start decorating your mini cakes! Here, we've used liquorice for Cookie's ears, and green jelly sweets for his eyes.

STEP 5

Using the squeezy black icing, carefully draw whiskers onto your Cookie mini cake. Once decorated, put your mini cakes back into the fridge until the chocolate is set.

STEP 6

Now let your creativity run riot and create as many different faces as you want! For doggy shapes, roll the balls into more of a rounded L-shape. Use yellow icing for blonde hair, and different colour chocolate for different skin tones. The choice is yours!

CELEB GUEST: HARRY HILL

FACTBYTES:

FULL NAME: Dr Matthew Keith Hall
JOB: Comedian and, er, ex-doctor
DOB: 1 October 1964

ON BLUE PETER:
Harry gave Joel a joke masterclass

HE TOLD US:
- I've got a four-chambered heart [but then so do all of us...]
- I remember jokes by knowing how people will laugh at them

BET YOU DIDN'T KNOW:
A man went into a fish and chip shop and asked for a piece of cod. The man behind the counter said, "OK, sir, it won't be long". The other man said, "Well, it'd better be thick then"!

ON HIS JOB:
"I started out as a doctor, but had this feeling I didn't really know what was going on. In most walks of life that doesn't matter. If you're a doctor it's probably quite important."

WHEN HE WAS YOUNGER:
"My advice for telling jokes at school would be to work up a little routine. Always open with your best joke - that way you get them in. Close with your second best joke. Maybe stand on a little box as well, and get someone with a torch to shine it in your face."

"If it's going badly, get off. If it's going well, get off. Always leave them wanting more. And have fun!"

CELEB GUESTS: JONAS BROTHERS

Joe: "The best thing is meeting fans personally, touring the world and playing music. Just doing what we love."

FACTBYTES:

KEVIN'S FULL NAME: Paul Kevin Jonas II
JOB: Lead guitar and backing vocals
DOB: 5 November 1987

JOE'S FULL NAME: Joseph Adam Jonas
JOB: Lead vocals and guitar
DOB: 15 August 1989

NICK'S FULL NAME: Nicholas Jerry Jonas
JOB: Lead vocals, guitar and drums
DOB: 16 September 1992

ON BLUE PETER:
They answered questions sent in by Blue Peter viewers

THEY TOLD US:
- If we could have any superpower, Kevin would fly, and Joe would shoot bacon out of his eyes. (?!)
- Nick would be an athlete if he wasn't a singer

BET YOU DIDN'T KNOW:
They'd love to work with 80s popster Prince, who's a huge influence on them.

WHEN HE WAS YOUNGER:
Nick: "I only started playing drums when I was about 11, and it's just a lot of fun. I'd say just keep on practising."

IT'S A TOUGH JOB*...

CATAMARAN CAPTAIN

"Let's see what this does!"

This beast needed taming, and we knew just the person for the job - Helen. She had the task of captaining the state-of-the-art "Condor Vitesse" catamaran right across the English Channel. Her jobs included directing the cars onto the ship, welcoming passengers onto the ship - and steering it.

FACTBYTE

The catamaran carries 700 passengers and 200 cars!

SCHOOL FIRE FIGHTER

Your lessons might get interrupted for all kinds of reasons, but perhaps not to put out a fire! Gordonstoun School in northern Scotland is the only one in the country where the students have their own fire service, complete with two fire engines. Helen joined their training, before taking part in a live drill (successfully, of course!).

"Now this is fun"

*BUT SOMEBODY'S GOT TO DO IT

BAND MANAGER

When Joel first joined Blue Peter, all he could talk about was how much he liked The Saturdays. So we fixed it for him to manage them for a day, taking them around rehearsals, radio stations and an MTV performance. Only things ran late in make-up, he screwed up their lunch order, and they didn't quite get his jokes. So the fact that they were still smiling at the end is a miracle!

Joel absolutely loves films, and celebs, and kids' gadgets, so when the chance came up to help set up the Transformers 2 premiere, he was straight in there! The preparations included rolling out the red (well, blue) carpet. Most of all, though, Joel somehow found a need to talk endlessly to Shia LaBeouf and Megan Fox. Wonder why?

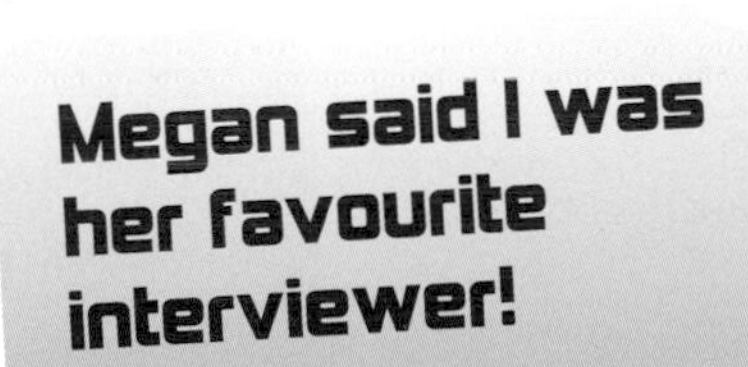

ANDY'S FLUORESCENT JACKET

OK, so a pattern seems to have emerged: Andy appears to have done more of the tough jobs than either of the other two. And we don't mean "showbiz" tough like Joel – we're talking bin man, sewage cleaner-upper, white line painter and 999 operator. All vital roles, of course, and ones which Andy totally threw himself into. But next year, maybe we'll try to up Andy's glamour count...!

JOEL'S JOURNEY

BEING A BLUE PETER PRESENTER IS A LOT ABOUT ACTION, ADVENTURE, CHALLENGES, MEETING CELEBS AND HAVING FUN. OCCASIONALLY, THOUGH, SOMETHING COMES UP WHICH IS TOTALLY DIFFERENT. THIS WAS ONE OF THOSE MOMENTS. AND IT'S PROBABLY CHANGED MY LIFE.

I'm Jewish, which means I was born into a family that follows the Jewish religion. But I have never really followed my faith: I haven't gone to synagogue, prayed very much, eaten kosher food, that kind of thing.

My Grandad was very different. His Jewish beliefs were vital to him, and he always used to ask me to find out more about my Jewish background. But he died last year - before I could even tell him I'd become a Blue Peter presenter. So now I'm doing what he always wanted me to do. This is for you, Grandad.

I began by getting on a webcam to my Grandma, who now lives in New Zealand. Talking about it all hit me very hard. If you read last year's Blue Peter Annual, you'll know I said I wanted to find out if anything would affect me enough that I'd cry on camera. I cried on camera that day.

Me, aged 9, with my Grandad and Grandma.

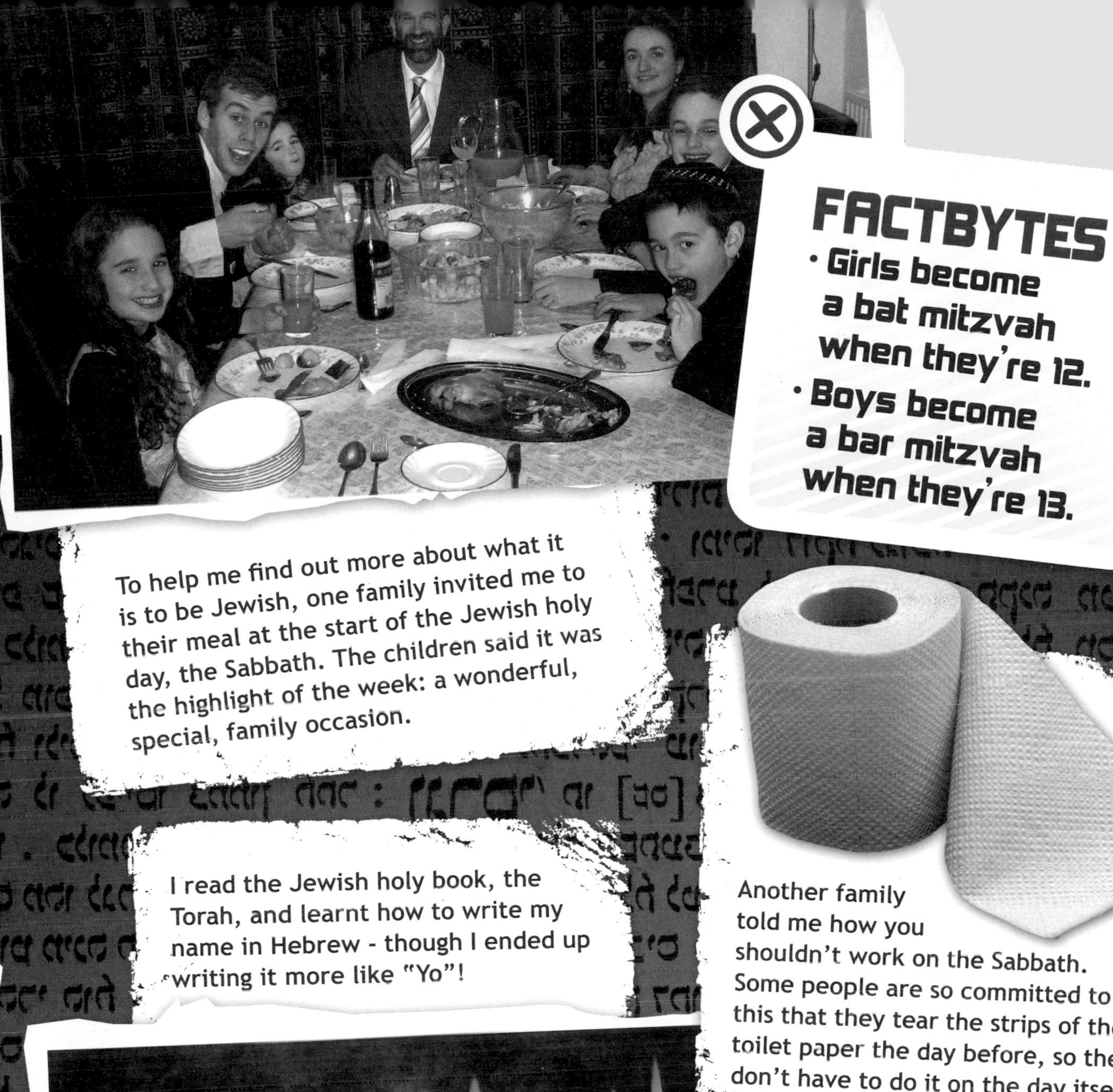

FACTBYTES

- Girls become a bat mitzvah when they're 12.
- Boys become a bar mitzvah when they're 13.

To help me find out more about what it is to be Jewish, one family invited me to their meal at the start of the Jewish holy day, the Sabbath. The children said it was the highlight of the week: a wonderful, special, family occasion.

I read the Jewish holy book, the Torah, and learnt how to write my name in Hebrew - though I ended up writing it more like "Yo"!

Another family told me how you shouldn't work on the Sabbath. Some people are so committed to this that they tear the strips of their toilet paper the day before, so they don't have to do it on the day itself!

And I was lucky enough to attend a "bat mitzvah" celebration, when a Jewish girl passes into adulthood. It was an emotional and powerful occasion. I could see why people care so deeply about their faith.

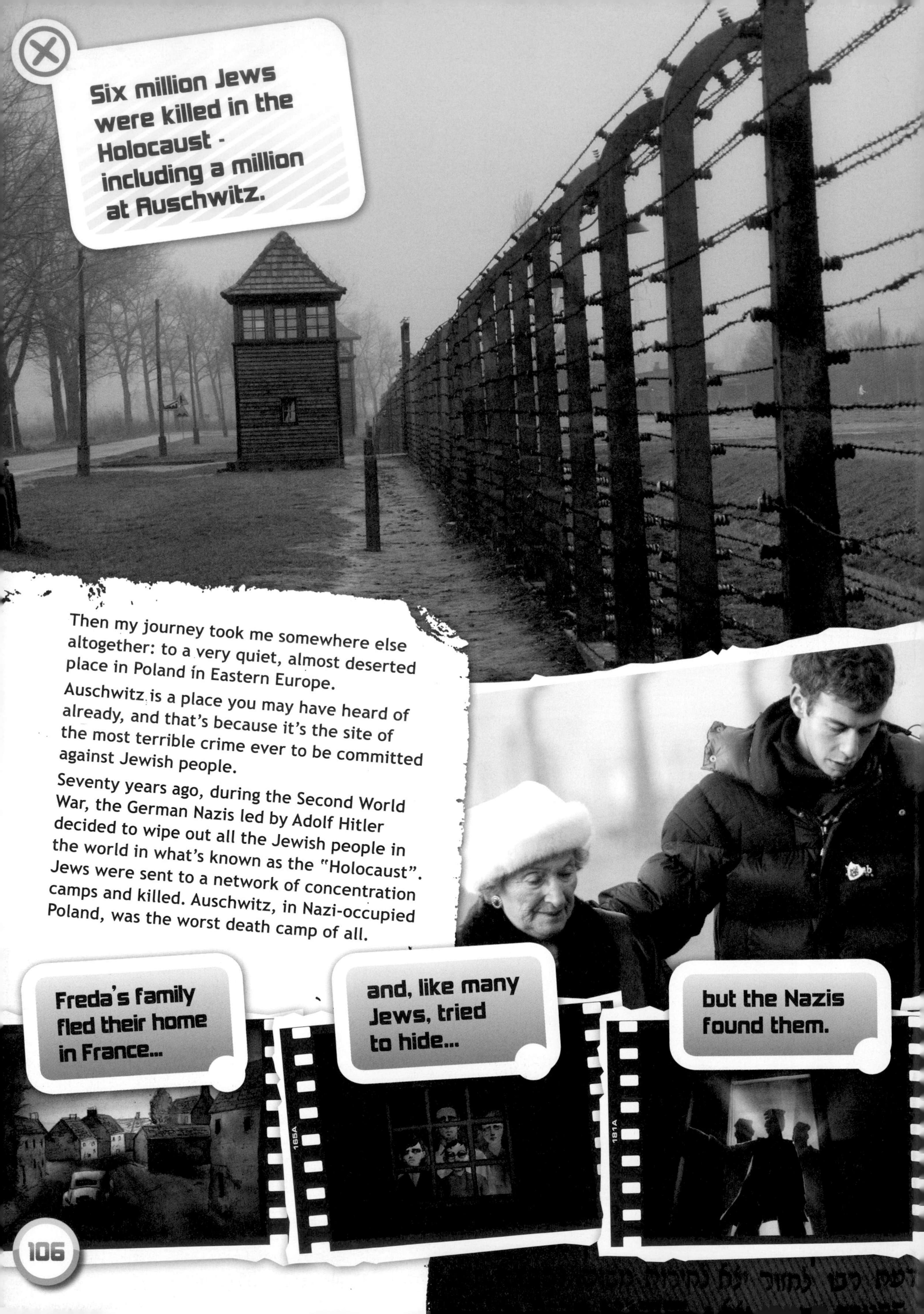

Then my journey took me somewhere else altogether: to a very quiet, almost deserted place in Poland in Eastern Europe.

Auschwitz is a place you may have heard of already, and that's because it's the site of the most terrible crime ever to be committed against Jewish people.

Seventy years ago, during the Second World War, the German Nazis led by Adolf Hitler decided to wipe out all the Jewish people in the world in what's known as the "Holocaust". Jews were sent to a network of concentration camps and killed. Auschwitz, in Nazi-occupied Poland, was the worst death camp of all.

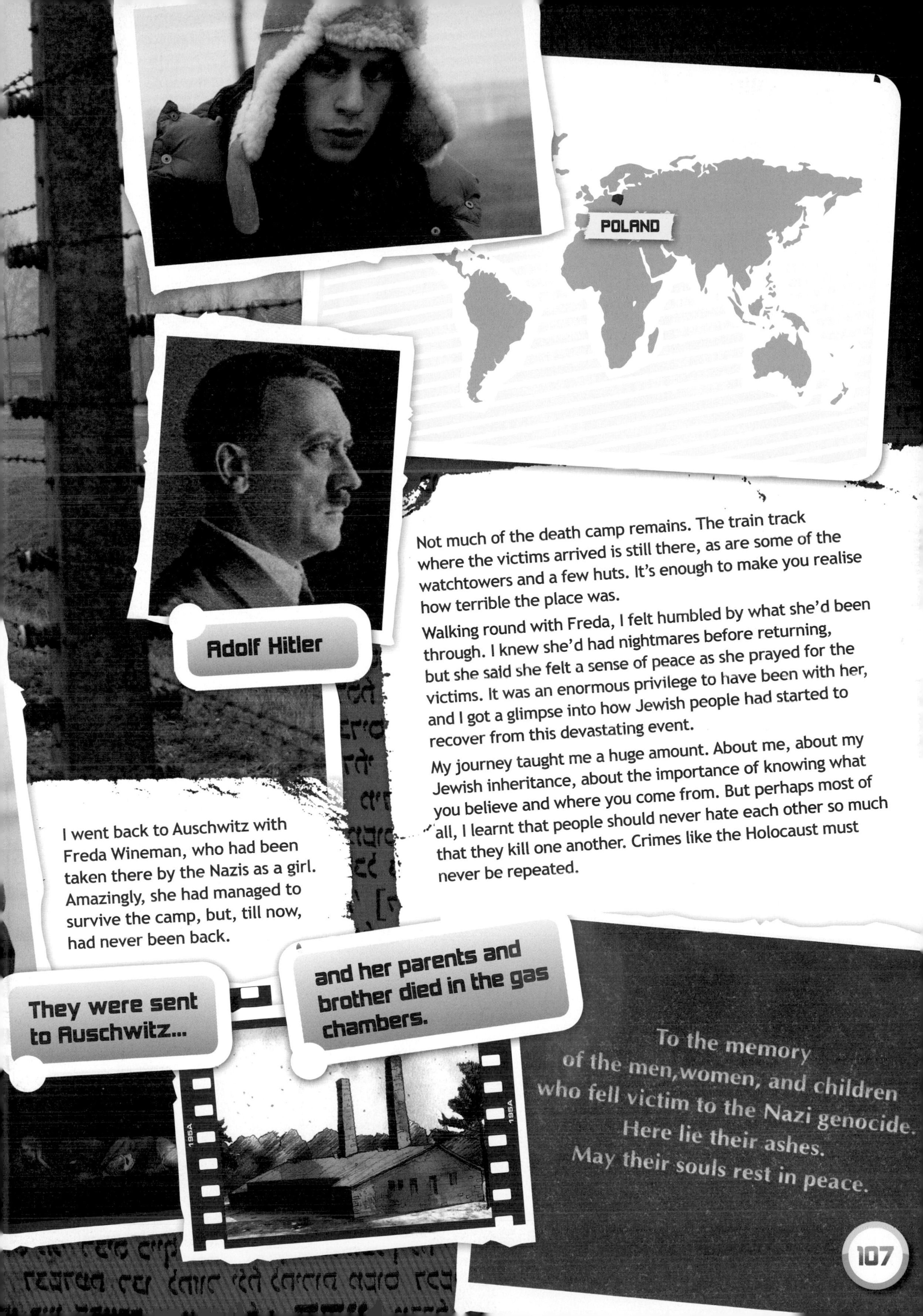

I went back to Auschwitz with Freda Wineman, who had been taken there by the Nazis as a girl. Amazingly, she had managed to survive the camp, but, till now, had never been back.

Not much of the death camp remains. The train track where the victims arrived is still there, as are some of the watchtowers and a few huts. It's enough to make you realise how terrible the place was.

Walking round with Freda, I felt humbled by what she'd been through. I knew she'd had nightmares before returning, but she said she felt a sense of peace as she prayed for the victims. It was an enormous privilege to have been with her, and I got a glimpse into how Jewish people had started to recover from this devastating event.

My journey taught me a huge amount. About me, about my Jewish inheritance, about the importance of knowing what you believe and where you come from. But perhaps most of all, I learnt that people should never hate each other so much that they kill one another. Crimes like the Holocaust must never be repeated.

WHERE'S WALLY?

For our 50th birthday a whole load of people helped us celebrate - including legendary children's character Wally. Martin Handford, who draws every Where's Wally illustration, very kindly made us a special one-off edition of his famous creation.

WHICH LEAVES ONLY ONE QUESTION. CAN YOU FIND WALLY?

Martin drawing Wally and his friends

"If you can do this, you're a whole load cleverer than me!"

FACTBYTES

- More than 73 million copies of the Where's Wally books have been sold in over 50 countries!
- Each picture can take up to eight weeks to draw

In these exclusive "making of" images, you can see how carefully the illustration came together

TIP: Use a magnifying glass if you get stuck!

HAPPY 50TH BIRTHDAY

BLUE PETER

QUIZ ANSWERS

NOT-SO-CROSS WORD (PAGE 9)

SPOT THE DIFFERENCE (PAGE 24)

WORD SEARCH CELEBS (PAGE 25)

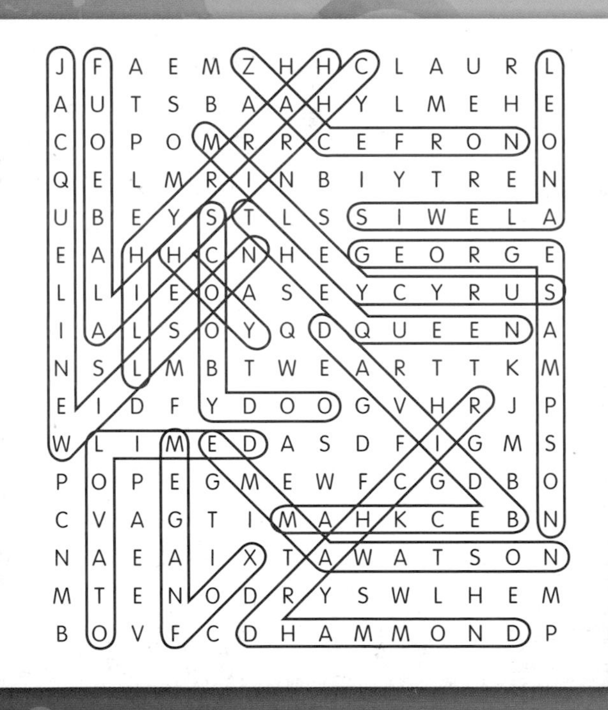

BLUE PETER SUPERQUIZ

ROUND 1 (PAGE 22)

1: A, 2: A, 3: B, 4: Cumbria, 5: B, 6: B, 7: C, 8: B, 9: A, 10: A. Your total:

ROUND 2 (PAGE 48)

1: C, 2: A, 3: C, 4: B, 5: London, 6: B, 7: A, 8: A, 9: B, 10: No. Your total:

ROUND 3 (PAGE 70)

1: B, 2: B, 3: B, 4: A, 5: A, 6: Me, 7: B, 8: Nigeria, 9: B, 10: A. Your total:

ROUND 4 (PAGE 94)

1: A, 2: I'm a rescue dog, 3: A, 4: A, 5: A, 6: B, 7: C, 8: C, 9: C, 10: A. Your total:

Add all four totals together and write your final score out of 40 points here:

0-10 POINTS: TIN FOIL

Did you actually watch any Blue Peter this year?

11-20 POINTS: BRONZE

Not bad. I suppose it's the taking part that counts.

21-30 POINTS: SILVER

Pretty impressive. You're on the ball. We like you!

31-40 POINTS: GOLD!

Amazing! Words fail us! Have you thought of being Prime Minister one day?!

MY TRICKY TRACK (PAGE 35)

1. Namibia; 2. Athens; 3. Silver; 4. Relay; 5. Yellow; 6. Walking; 7. Go; 8. Ohuruogu; 9. Ultra; 10. Athletics; 11. Sun.

My ideal next ultimate challenge would be EVEREST.

BADGE BONANZA (PAGE 50)

1. LEGOLAND; 2. SEALIFE CENTRE; 3. CHESTER ZOO; 4. EDEN PROJECT; 5. TELEVISION CENTRE; 6. BEATRIX POTTER; 7. TOWER OF LONDON; 8. WARWICK CASTLE; 9. MONKEY WORLD; 10. ROALD DAHL; 11. MADAME TUSSAUDS.

The top-rated badge attraction is ALTON TOWERS.